HOW TO BE A FIRST-RATE FIRST MATE

HOW TO BE A FIRST-RATE FIRST MATE

A SAILING GUIDE FOR WOMEN

GLORIA SLOANE AND PHYLLIS COE

Edited by Don Stern

Quadrangle/The New York Times Book Co.

Library of Congress Catalog Card Number: 73-90171

International Standard Book Number: 0-8129- 0423-0

Book design: June Negrycz

CONTENTS

SECTION IV   GETTING IT ALL TOGETHER

SECTION V   KEEPING IT ALL TOGETHER

SECTION VI   IN THE WAKE

PREFACE

There *is* an easier way to do it!

It's called boatkeeping, the art of putting your boat in order and keeping it that way for months of cruising pleasure. In the galley the art lies in turning out appetizing meals in cramped quarters and the care and feeding of drop-in guests on short notice without short tempers. Topside, the trick is in handling all chores comfortably and helping the skipper run a tight ship.

The know-how for the easy way to do all of this is in this factual guide, through quick, reliable checklists that answer common boating problems faced by every boating gal . . . the panicky beginner or the experienced boat mate.

Once you've learned the easy way, you'll have more time for the magic moments of pure delight aboard a happy ship . . . a cup of hot bouillon after a swim on a crisp day . . . sun-warmed decks, soft pillows, and an offshore breeze . . . cocktails at sunset with opalescent water and sky . . . a racing wake . . . the taste of freshly caught grilled fish. . . .

If you are still doing it the hard way, turn the page and cast off!

THE SKIPPER'S DECALOGUE

*Or a Word to the Wives
is Sufficient*

1. I am the Skipper; thou shalt question not that which I do nor that which I say.

2. Thou shalt not expect me to be available for whatsoever hath not concern with boating, such as bridge, golf, movies, or car trips.

3. Thou shalt never question moneys spent on paint, chroming, canvas, equipment, or anything pertaining to boating.

4. Thou shalt cease to expect fur coats, new furniture, rugs, and even more essential commodities, until the boating budget has a surplus . . . if even never.

5. Thou shalt expect not thy Skipper to busy himself with mowing the lawn, plucking the weeds, repairing the house, nor any labor other than the maintenance of his boat.

6. Thou shalt prepare thyself to be a worthy mate aboard—to be a chef in the galley, a hostess in the lounge, and a deckhand on a cruise.

7. Thou shalt occupy uncomplainingly the hard bunk, I the soft one.

8. Thou shalt before inviting guests aboard beseech thy Skipper's permission, and invitest only those whom he approves; whereupon it becomes thy duty to see that they come aboard appropriately shod for treading on decks.

9. Thou shalt jump when I say "Jump" and sit when I say "Sit"; thy summers shalt thou devote to my bidding, and thy winters to tolerating a basement filled with boating gear around which thy laundry shalt thou hang (since thou canst afford not a dryer).

10. Thou shalt expound forever the joys of boating, whilst casting adoring glances at thy Skipper, never uttering the sacrifices thou thinkest in thy weakmindedness that it doth involve; and if thou do all these things thou shalt be my dearest first mate for all my days. Selah.

—Betty Stockless

AN OUNCE OF PREVENTION

EXPECTANT BOATHOOD

Boating is an exciting, different way of life. It brings adventure, freedom from crowds, and all the comforts of home. How else could you get away with the whole family with the ease of pick-up-and-go and no traffic to buck? It's a tall order to fill; maybe that's why boating is so popular.

Until a few years ago it was the man's prerogative to make every last decision connected with *his* boat. But we've come a long way. Now it's a family affair and a skipper needs his mate and knows that the extras are important. After years of kowtowing to the masculine image of the hardy seafarer, boatbuilders have begun to consider the forgotten female. Decorators and consultants are busy measuring and designing with *you* in mind. You can look forward to a more luxurious boating life than old-timers ever dreamed possible.

The first step toward the good life is choosing your boat as carefully as you chose your home. The boat must fit your needs and carry all the extras that you can squeeze aboard. But it may be a far cry from the one your skipper would pick out on his own. It's a good bet that if he goes boat hunting alone, he'll come back with the soundest hull ever built, purring engines with 3-to-1 reduction gears, constavolts, and four extra spotlights. If he bothers to glance into the cabin at all, the sight of a single-burner stove and a couple of bunks will convince him that this is just the boat for you!

So, as soon as you catch that boatlust gleam in his eye, go along on the shopping expeditions. That's the time to look and learn. Later you'll be able to play an important part in the final decision by helping him buy a boat that *you* can live with comfortably as well as one *he* feels is the most seaworthy.

POWER OR SAIL

Whether to go into power or sail will be your very first decision. It is a personal matter of choice and very strong feelings, so don't look for objective guidelines here. Sailors look down on "stinkpots," while powerboat people fume at tacking sailboats that get in the way. Usually power people are the restless ones, anxious to see things and explore. Sailors don't care *where* they're going as long as they are on the water; it's the getting there that counts. Decide which is your way of life, and then go on to consider the other important factors.

HOW WILL YOU USE THE BOAT?

- How much time will you spend aboard? If you have a good deal of leisure time, you will want a boat with a wide cruising range, one that is comfortably fitted out for extended trips. If you use the boat only for fishing, skiing, and day trips, a smaller, simpler one will fit the bill.
- How long is the boating season in your area? Obviously a short season doesn't warrant a large investment. You may

decide to charter a boat and save yourself a large cash out-
lay.

- Where will you be using the boat? You need a sturdier craft
  on a large, open body of water than on a protected lake or
  bay. Here, your first thought is for safety.
- How many people do you plan to accommodate? The immediate family, of course, but what about the guests you'd
  like to invite along?
- What can you afford? Don't get carried away by a spank-
  ing-new boat and get in over your head. You may get better
  value in a good used boat.
- Will the boat grow with you and fulfill your needs over the
  next few years? Trading up is every boatman's disease.
  Consider all the above points so you won't have to trade too
  soon.

LOOK FOR COMFORT

If this is your first boat, you have a lot to learn before you
buy. An old hand has an easier time. She knows what she
had to put up with on the last boat and won't get stuck a second time! For comfort, look carefully at:

Galley.   Do you have enough facilities to make your job
easier? Will it efficiently stock enough to feed your crew?

Head.   Does it provide privacy?

Sleeping accommodations.   Sure, you'd like a bunk for
every member of the family, but is it really necessary?
The cockpit bench or a sleeping bag on deck can be second heaven for the kids.

Elbow room.   Will you all be able to stretch out comfortably and move around with a minimum of colliding?
"Mess time" will be just that if you are constantly bumping elbows.

Stowage.   Is there room for household gear, personal
items, and special recreational equipment? Remember,
too, that you are required by law to carry certain safety
items according to the size of the boat.

FITTING OUT

Fitting out is that busy time when the whine of the saw and the slap of paintbrush in boat yards and back yards announce that boat owners are putting their crafts in trim.

To some it is the time for grandiose dreams . . . a new depth finder, an automatic pilot, or, maybe, a generator. To others it is simply the moment to splash on a coat of paint and change the paper towels!

Let's face it; fitting out is just another name for spring cleaning and that always means elbow grease. But cheer up—it comes but once a year.

For northerners who haul their boats for the winter, fitting out really began last fall when they put the boat under canvas. If everything was thoroughly cleaned and left in good order, protected against winter dampness, they are well ahead. For warmer climates with a year-round season, it's important to keep out front so that a midseason turnout is fast and easy.

The preparations you make will see you through an entire boating season. If you do it once and do it right, you won't spend half your time in port awaiting repairs.

THREE BASIC RULES

1. Don't waste time sprucing up gear that must be over-hauled or replaced. See that it is in working order before you clean.
2. Don't struggle with a job that is too technical for you. If you find you can't get the stove to work properly, call in an expert before you gum up the works.
3. Divide the work sensibly. Most men feel that the engines and working parts are their special domain, but that still leaves plenty of chores for the crew. Review your lists, making sure that everybody, especially the children, has something to do. The chores they willingly accept will stun you.

FITTING-OUT CHECKLISTS

Below decks is the woman's world, but most skippers welcome help on topside jobs. Before the boat goes back into the water either for the summer or after a paint job, you can help:

- Inspect the condition of the hull and keel.
- Look for signs of dry rot (for remedies, see p. 15).
- Examine for damaged wood on the exterior.
- Check seams on deck and hull to see if caulking is needed.
- The hull and topsides must be painted every year; that's the skipper's domain but he very well may need help (see p. 127).
- Fiber-glass boats require a thorough washing and then a coat of wax to the hull.

⎈ AFTER LAUNCHING

On Deck

- Examine all lines and fenders; repair or replace those that have rotted or frayed.
- Look for rust or pitting on metal deck fixtures; polish as needed.
- Check for split cushion seams on the seats.
- Test the life preservers. Repair or replace those that show any sign of fraying or rotting.
- Inflate and test life rafts; toss the ring buoy and floating cushions into the water to check buoyancy.
- Be sure that all fire extinguishers are full and in working order.
- Check the screws in the stanchion bases. Loose screws are the prime source of leaks into the interior of the boat.
- Clean the sheets at home. Zip them into a nylon mesh bag to keep them from snarling in your washing machine.

Below Decks

- Examine all portholes, ventilators, and hatches for signs of leaks and dry rot.
- Are the sinks, handles, and faucets free of rust and leaks?
- Hook up the head and flush it with detergent and water.
- Check for leaks.
- Inspect the stove and the ice unit for frayed wires and loose connections. Refer to the manufacturer's manual for specific maintenance instructions.
- Check for loose electrical connections and frayed wires.
- Fitting-out time is the logical moment to paint or varnish the cabin interior if it's needed (see p. 127 for instructions).

⎈ SCRUBBING UP

Now that you've put everything in working order and in its place, it's time to scrub up. You'll need:

- **A light vacuum cleaner with a long extension cord:** Most marinas provide electrical outlets on the dock, so you may want to buy and keep a small vacuum for use aboard.
- **Some useful cleaners:** washing soda, household ammonia, all-purpose detergent, spray glass cleansers, rust removers, metal polish, vinegar, and teak cleaner.
- **Cleaning tools:** a hose, a pail, a mop, clean rags, sponges, steel wool, scrub brushes of varying sizes (including a toothbrush for tough corners), a chamois cloth, and paper towels.
- **Miscellaneous:** all-purpose lubricating oil, mildew spray, and the ever-present notebook and pencil for lists.

Topside First

- Hose the decks and cockpit; then scrub thoroughly with water and a mild detergent. A too-strong solution will damage the paint.
- For teak decks and fittings, use teak cleanser only.
- Scrub metals with steel wool or use rust remover where necessary; then apply the all-purpose polish.
- Clean deck cushions with detergent and water.
- Polish the instrument panel.
- Wash the windshield.

On to the Interior

- Fill the fresh-water tanks.
- Take the mattresses, curtains, and cushions topside for airing.
- Start forward and clean your way aft, working over floors, bulkheads, hanging lockers, cubbies, and storage chests.
- Wash walls, in sections, from the top down; rinse as you go. Use water sparingly to prevent dirty rivulets from running and smearing.

- Apply a strong solution of vinegar and water to dark and damp areas where mildew breeds; follow up with an anti-mildew spray.
- Use washing soda and water on painted surfaces to remove the dirt but not the paint.
- Maneuver your vacuum extension to reach hard-to-get corners.
- Clean portholes and windows with window spray or a solution of ammonia and water. Use horizontal strokes on one side and vertical strokes on the other to show up the smudges. Salt-laden air may build up several layers of dirt and salt, so a second cleaning may be necessary.
- A slightly dampened chamois cloth will bring out the soft, natural gloss of varnished wood finishes.
- Oil all hinges. If you run out of oil, substitute petroleum jelly or cooking oil.
- Remove rust from door handles, switch plates, faucet handles, drawer pulls, and pipes with steel wool or rust remover; then polish. Add a fresh coat of aluminum paint to pipes to retard rust.

Finally, the Galley

- Flush the sink and drains.
- Scrub the refrigerator or ice box with a mixture of washing soda and warm water. Pour some through the drains.
- Wash the eating and cooking utensils, pots and pans, and dishes.
- Scrub drawers and cubbies.
- Check any leftover supplies.

Now the scutwork is over and everything is shipshape. It's time to bring your gear back aboard and stow it in clean lockers. You are well fitted out, and the days of fishing, swimming, and cruising are just ahead.

(

BOATKEEPING

Imagine visiting a yard where two identical cruisers— same builder, model and year— are tied up side by side. The first boat looks old and neglected, while the other has gleaming varnish, has decks cleared for action, and seems spanking new as well as several lovely feet longer. You might never recognize them as sister ships.

This dramatic—and unlikely—situation points up the fact that some boats always seem "yachty" while others look tired and worn. The explanation has nothing to do with the amounts of money spent on upkeep or heavy-duty cruising; it lies in pride of possession and tender loving care.

Call it boatkeeping or preventative maintenance; it all adds up to extra attention to detail and a sensible daily routine. Together they guarantee trouble-free cruising and a trim ship. The goal is to keep ahead of trouble without scrubbing your days away.

⊕ AN OUNCE OF PREVENTION

- Freshen your brightwork with an extra midseason coat of varnish (see p. 130). A daily rub with a damp chamois cloth will keep it beautiful.
- At least once during the heavy cruising season, turn out cubbies, drawers, and lockers. Look for oily rags or mildew.
- Periodically check that the fire extinguishers are full and in working order.
- As you use them, check all your sockets and plugs. Damp air works its way into little corners.
- Maintain the shine on faucets and hardware—rust and pitting sneak in fast.
- Regularly flush the drains of the ice unit and galley sink. Wash with warm suds and follow with a soda rinse to keep them sweet.
- Clean your stove daily to prevent dangerous grease buildup.
- Once a week, flush cleanser through the head.
- Use disposable paper towels for cleaning jobs. Cloth rags have a nasty way of piling up.
- Securely wrap portable radios, TV, and phonographs and their spare batteries in plastic bags when they are not in use. Dampness quickly erodes their tiny wires.
- Insist that everyone pick up his clutter. There isn't room for untidiness, and it could be a hazard.
- To get rid of seasick odors, wash the area with either a solution of baking soda and water or with club soda straight out of the bottle. Vinegar also does the trick.

⊕ LAUNDRY

Laundry poses no problems on a weekend cruise, but on longer trips it's a nuisance. If there are no washing machines at the marina, take the laundry to the laundromat in town when you shop or go sightseeing. Some marinas can supply the names of local laundries that offer special fast service to visiting boats. If you have to do it yourself, *never*

wash in salt water—the salt crystals absorb night dampness or morning dew. On a rainy day put your towels and
bathing suits out on deck for a fresh-water rinse.

⚓ ON LEAVING THE BOAT

- Empty the icebox and throw away everything that might
  spoil. Dispose of that last little chunk of ice and leave the
  door or lid ajar.
- Be sure the valves on the stove are tightly closed.
- Flush the head with cleanser and leave some in the drain.
- Leave doors and drawers ajar for ventilation.
- Collect the laundry and the inevitable clutter for the trip
  home.
- If you use the boat only on weekend outings, don't leave the
  bunks made up with linens while you are away. They will
  feel damp and limp when you return. Make them up fresh
  each time.
- Keep a checklist of all supplies to be replaced. Take it with
  you whenever you go ashore and pick up replacements
  promptly.
- Always lock your boat; vandals are not exclusively a city
  problem. If you like, leave the key at the marina office in
  case of emergency.

⚓ DRY ROT AND MILDEW

Dampness, not dirt, is the chief enemy aboard. Not only
does it pit and rust metals, but fresh-water puddles cause
dry rot that attacks wood; add salt spray and you have mildew that attacks anything but synthetic fibers.

Dry rot is a fungus that leaves spongy, soft areas that become powdery when dry. The affected area has no resist-
ance to pressure; a pointed tool penetrates easily. It spreads
rapidly and is a serious hazard. To prevent dry rot you
must promptly attend to leaks from rain and your own
fresh-water washdowns, particularly around hatches and

portholes and in open seams. In the galley the spots to watch are the spaces under and around the sink and ice unit drains. Never leave puddles; mop them as you go.

The surest treatment for dry rot is to cut it out, cover the surrounding area with a preservative, and replace with new wood. Some preparations on the market will cure small areas; injected directly into the affected section with a hypodermic needle or through small holes drilled nearby, they soak the area by capillary action, harden the wood and, destroy the fungus. This cure is not guaranteed, so use it below deck and not on the hull or other sections that must remain structurally sound.

Mildew is another spore-producing fungus. It resembles green, black, or white mold and needs darkness, stagnant air, moisture, or heat to start on its insidious path. Fabrics become discolored, and you are left with a musty, spoiled, and unpleasant odor. In extreme cases, mildew rots fabrics completely.

To Guard Against Mildew

- Vent all locker doors and drawers with cut-out slits to facilitate air circulation.
- Ventilate all areas where rope, canvas, or life preservers are stored.
- Place packets of calcium chloride (or a half bar of soap left in its wrapper) in enclosed spaces to soak up dampness.
- Spray antimildew aerosol liberally and often on mattresses, curtains, and all fabrics.
- After a rainy spell, air drawers and lockers for an hour or two.
- Notch the clothes rods in hanging lockers to keep the hangers apart and allow for air circulation between garments.
- When you leave the boat, switch on a low-watt light bulb or plug an electric dehumidifier into the dockside outlet to keep the air dry.

LAYING UP FOR THE WINTER

In colder climates putting the boat under canvas for the winter is as important but not so strenuous as spring fitting out.

- If you have the storage room, take home all removable curtains, pillows, linens, lamps, and accessories for dry winter storage.
- Air and thoroughly dry all fabrics that you cannot remove. Wrap them in large plastic bags.
- Treat mattresses and permanent seat covers with an anti-mildew spray. Stand mattresses on their sides for maximum air circulation.
- Leave hatches, drawers, and appliance doors open for ventilation.
- Clean and disconnect the stove and refrigerator.
- Remove *all* food and beverages from the galley. If left aboard, cans and steel wool pads rust, and liquid-filled containers can freeze and burst.
- Drain the water storage tank; frozen water expands and may damage the tank.
- Coat all metal surfaces with petroleum jelly, grease, or cooking oil to retard rusting and pitting.
- BUT leave the fire extinguishers aboard. Fires in storage sheds or under canvas are not unknown. Whoever is first on the scene will need the apparatus.

 MAINTENANCE IN MODERATION

Some slaveys get so carried away by the expression "seagoing and Bristol fashion" that they spend all their time cleaning and never get to leave the dock. Think of these checklists as reminders of chores to be done regularly, not compulsively!

A PLACE FOR EVERYTHING AND...

DECORATING

Your boat is a vacation home—a place to relax in comfort on weekends and extended trips. It truly becomes a "pleasure boat" when you take your comforts to sea.

Comfort comes in many forms—room to spread out makeup when you dress for dinner ashore, cubby space for extra towels, scatter pillows to tuck under your back, and a cozy, cheerful cabin on a rainy day.

No boat can carry all the little things that add up to pure luxury; you must choose what is most important to you and your family. Use every clever decorating trick you know (and make up a few) to meet the space challenge. Use color to make your cabins seem roomier, and find ways and means to easy maintenance. You'll be surprised how much you can do.

⚓ STORAGE ON DECK

There are always a million things to be stowed. Unless you want your precious cabin cubbies to overflow with bilge pumps and a deluge of spare parts, start solving your storage problems by finding room for the skipper's gear topside where it belongs.

- Enclose the open space beneath the built-in bench with sliding plywood doors to make an extra storage bin.
- Or search the unpainted furniture stores for small, inexpensive cabinets to fit into the same area. Paint or varnish them to match.
- Install small shelves and hooks to organize the contents and double the capacity of the new compartments. Try the same trick under the cockpit seats on sailboats.
- Hang narrow racks with guard rails around the sides of the cockpit to hold small elusive gadgets.
- Put up plastic-coated, rust-resistant cup hooks in the cockpit to hang towels and ditty bags—filled with combs, tissues, and lotions—out of the way.
- Stack and enclose the life preservers in a square, zippered canvas or nylon case. These are available at most boating supply stores. Use them as extra seats on deck and save locker space.

⚓ CABIN STORAGE

Wise use of space in the cabin can add to your comfort and convenience.

- Stretch inches of space into a storage wall by building shelves with guard (pew) rails into the open spaces between the exposed ribs on the bulkheads. The shelves, never more than two or three inches deep, can hold magazines, books, cameras, and all the "things" that clutter. Make a practical bar by spacing a few of the pew rails high enough above the shelves to secure bottles and glasses.

Storage Wall

- Enclose space under steps as either drawers or cubbies.
- If there is wasted space over a built-in chest, use it for a rack or cabinet bolted to the bulkhead.
- During the day keep linens for main cabin sleeping accommodations out of the cubbies and rolled into pillow shams.

CREATE ILLUSION WITH COLOR

Even the cabins of a luxury liner are made for compact living. So you have a lot more stretching to do on your pocket cruiser! You can't actually create space out of thin air but you can create that illusion with imaginative use of fabrics and paint.

Color and Paint

- Bring reflected sunlight from the water into the cabin by painting walls and ceilings with light, cool shades of semi-gloss or high-gloss enamel. Besides catching the light, enamel paints are easy to clean with a swipe of a cloth.
- Contrasting trim creates a dramatic effect in a good-sized room, but in a crowded cabin it brings the walls in on you. Unless you have varnished hatches and portholes, paint them the same colors as the bulkheads.
- Don't clutter the bulkheads with assorted nautical gear. The "busy" effect makes a small cabin seem even tinier.
- Fade cabinets into the background by again using the same wall colors.
- Light colors on the insides of drawers, cabinets, and lockers make it easier to spot small objects.

Carefree, Colorful Fabrics

Fabrics also help create a feeling of lightness and space. There is a wide range of vinyls, Naugahydes, plastics, synthetics, and spun-glass fabrics in solids, patterns, and textures that are durable and easy to clean.

- On deck or in the cabin buy only materials that are both water-repellent and resistant to mildew.
- Bring in the excitement of color contrast by using bright colors, but keep the variety to a minimum.
- Use small checks or patterns to create eye interest, or look for texture in fabrics to break up monotony.

Coordinate Your Colors

Paint and fabrics should do things for each other. Once you've chosen your paint, dab a few strokes of the color on a piece of white paper and take it with you when shopping for fabrics so that you can keep your color tones in key.

- If you like the outdoor look, you might choose fabrics in shades of lime and green against pale yellow walls and ceiling. For example, green tweed on the floor might be complemented with yellow and green scatter pillows, lamp shades, and ash trays.
- Another combination sets off white bulkheads with black or grey small-checked fabrics. The color scheme is completed with grey tweed rugs and bright red accessories.
- Pale blue walls, a white ceiling, and shades of deeper blues on the furniture and floor can all be perked up with white or red accessories.
- Pale yellow walls contrast vividly with brown on the seats and in the rug. Bright yellow or orange touches in the accessories are cheerful additions.

FURNITURE

Of course, most boat furniture is built-in, but in the main cabin of a larger boat there is occasional space for freestanding pieces. If you have the room, choose furniture with these points in mind:

- Before you shop; measure the space to be filled and the width of the hatch. You may not be able to get your treasure inside the cabin!
- Try for a light look with small-scale, wide-based furniture. Department and furniture stores carry a surprisingly wide selection of small, inexpensive pieces. Look for convertible furniture designed for small apartments, they solve the same space problems aboard.
- Check unpainted furniture shops for a good selection of small cabinets that you can color-match to the walls.
- Wicker furniture is cool and fresh when painted. The bases can be weighted.

- Modern furniture with its clean, trim lines adds a light look to a small cabin.
- Check the new line of inflatable plastic tables and chairs that disappear into a cubby when not in use.
- For safety's sake, select pieces with rounded edges. Sharp corners and angles make big gouges in shins. Look for recessed drawer and door pulls to spare the bumps and bruises.
- Deep ashtrays with nonskid bases and lamps bolted to bulkheads and table tops stay put in heavy seas.

 TABLES

Try to work a good-sized table into the cabin, not only for dining but as a chart table for the captain and a play space for active kids.

- A board that folds flat up against the bulkhead is the most adaptable table in a small area. Attach it to the bulkhead with piano hinges; when lowered for use, a removable leg fits into a peg hole on the underside to give it stability.
- If you have a little more space, look for small cocktail tables that convert into full dining size.
- For easy maintenance, install Formica tops on tables and counters.

FANCY FLOORING

- Over linoleum or vinyl floors, choose nonskid washable scatter rugs to keep wet feet from slipping.
- Indoor-outdoor carpeting comes in wall-to-wall sizes and also in removable squares so that stained portions can be lifted out and cleaned. It is mildew-resistant and has a heavy plastic backing to minimize engine noise.
- On land, wall-to-wall carpeting is the mark of the affluent, but on a boat it is surprisingly practical and relatively inexpensive because of the small areas involved.

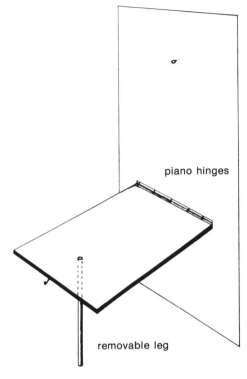

piano hinges

removable leg

A Fold-Down Table

- If you choose carpeting, don't tack it down. It must be easily removable. Cut it carefully to fit so that the edges won't curl.
- Put a foam rubber pad underneath to cut down noise from the engine.
- Choose a shaggy tweed to soak up wet-feet drippings, and put off carpet cleaning as long as possible.

PORTHOLE PRIVACY

With mobs of people constantly roaming the docks at a marina, you can feel as if you're living in a goldfish bowl. To insure some measure of privacy:

- Cover all portholes and windows with shades or curtains.
- Use spun-glass fabrics if you choose . . . they are light enough to offer privacy without shutting out air.
- Cover large windows with shades that roll up from the bottom and fasten with a hook at the top. It minimizes flapping.
- Be sure there are screens on all windows and portholes. That little cove might swarm with mosquitoes that come to visit as soon as you drop the anchor.

⚙ GALLEY TOUCHES

In older boats the galley area is just above the bilge, and you've got your work cut out to make it a pleasant work area. To help cheer it up:

- Keep your colors bright and light.
- If you redo the sink or counter areas, use either stainless steel or brightly colored Formica.
- Put down a colorful, nonskid scatter rug to provide a firm foothold on a rocky floor.
- Install a guard rail on the bulkhead or counter to steady yourself when the boat hits a big wave.
- Hinged boards hooked onto the bulkhead create more work space when lowered to rest on another counter.
- For extra work space, have a piece of plywood cut to fit over the sink when it is not in use.

⚙ STATEROOMS

A stateroom may be nothing more than V berths forward with a screening curtain, but it still deserves special attention.

- Buy mattresses and pillows of foam rubber and use drip-dry linens and blankets. They don't absorb the dampness and are resistant to mildew.

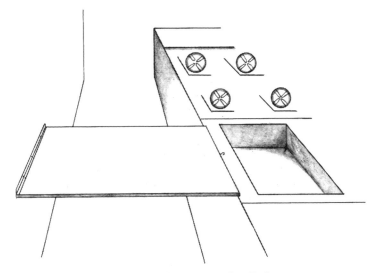

Extra Counter Space for the Galley

- Instead of ticking, cover bunk mattresses with cheerful synthetic fabrics, so morning chores will consist of folding and stowing linens or sleeping bags into pillow shams; the bunks can then become attractive settees for daytime lounging.
- Fasten small fish-net or pullman-type hammocks on the bulkheads at the head or side of the bunks for storing small personal items.
- Fit shallow, back-of-the-door cabinets (found in bath shops) to the inside of the stateroom door for additional cabinet space.

Linen

- Nothing beats contour sheets for bunk making. They are expensive when custom made, but you can easily make your own. Round the corners of a cot-sized sheet and gather and seam them with elastic. Go further and contour the bottoms of the top sheet and blanket as well.
- Because boat mattresses differ in size for each bunk, use in-

delible ink to mark each respective contour sheet and mattress.

- To turn an easily laundered synthetic quilt into a sleeping bag, fold it in half lengthwise, seam the bottom and put in a heavy-duty zipper three quarters of the way down the side.
- Flatten and store extra linens under the mattresses to save cubby space.
- Color-code your boat linens for easier sorting of laundry at home—and to make sure you remember to take them back!

⚓ HANGING LOCKERS

Even if your hanging locker is too tiny to deserve the name, you can organize it to hold just a little bit more:

- Buy hangers that hold more than one garment. There are combination jacket-and-skirt hangers and those that have arms to hold three or four pairs of slacks.
- Hang a shoe bag on the inside of the door. Buy the largest size that fits the door and use some of the pockets to store small items.
- Wire hangers rust quickly in salt air; to avoid stains on clothing use only plastic or wooden hangers.
- If the locker is full-sized, install two clothing racks, one near the top and one halfway down.

⚓ HEADS

If the cabins are crowded, the space reserved for the head is miniscule! Where you need space savers the most:

- Fit small, narrow pew shelves and extra medicine chests high up near the ceiling if possible.
- Perhaps you can enclose the base of the sink for extra storage.

- Save floor space by hanging a car litter bag instead of using an on-the-floor basket.
- Attach a hinged board (as described on p. 26) to the wall. Lower it when you need the room to spread out first-aid supplies or makeup.
- Install plastic nonrusting towel racks.
- For a final touch of luxury, put a full-length mirror on the door!

DON'T COOK UP IN A STORM

SECTION III

SETTING UP
YOUR GALLEY

Happily a galley is half the size, half the steps, and half the work of your kitchen at home. Even so, you'll want to be doubly efficient to satisfy those gargantuan sea appetites and still manage to spend most of your time topside.

MAKING ROOM

No great chef can function efficiently without all those handy thingamabobs that make cooking a snap, but there just isn't room to bring them all aboard. Still, you needn't settle for just the bare essentials. Look around; there's always a little cranny for another hook to hold one more gadget.

- Double the storage area in the cubbies by resetting the shelves closer together. Give yourself one 12-inch shelf for tall boxes and space the others 8 or 9 inches apart.

- Put up small shelves (with guard rails) for spices and condiments in the space between any exposed ribs on the sides of the boat. This is also the spot for your knife racks.
- Attach cup hooks to the ribs for cooking utensils, pot holders, and measuring cups. Set the hooks far enough apart to prevent the utensils from swinging together and jangling while the boat is under way.
- Fit metal spice racks on the insides of doors directly between the shelves. They will hold a dozen small items and cans.

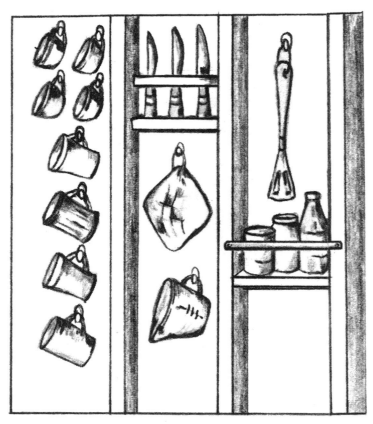

Galley Storage Wall

- Use plastic lazy-susan turntables to utilize the space in deep, hard-to-reach cubbies.
- To keep dishes out of lockers and leave room for foodstuffs, hang ready-made racks on the bulkheads for dishes, cups, and glassware.
- Stash your pots and pans in the oven when not in use.

⚓ COOL IT!

On a hot day there is a constant trek to the galley for ice-cold relief. But the heat and all-pervading dampness aboard a boat puts an extra strain on any refrigeration unit—portable cooler, permanent ice chest, or a luxurious refrigerator and freezer. To get maximum efficiency from your unit:

- Insist on heavy insulation in any unit you buy.
- Choose a unit with drains that are easily accessible for cleaning.
- Don't overload a chest. The ice or cooling mechanism dispels only so much cool air, and *all* items will spoil in a crowded box.
- Whenever possible, put the ice in the chest or turn on the refrigerator the day before you plan to use it so that it will be cold and ready for your food supplies.
- Pack the most perishable items first and closest to the ice.
- Do not open the unit unnecessarily. To cut down on the traffic, bring along a small portable ice chest, and fill it with cubes for cold drinks.
- When at anchor, you can hang a net bag with canned drinks over the side of the boat, and let the water keep them cool. But don't forget to pull up the net when you leave!
- Check your refrigerated foods every couple of days, mold develops more quickly at sea than at home.

WHAT KIND OF STOVE?

There are a dozen points of view when boat gals compare notes on the choice of a boat stove, but all agree that a single burner won't do much except cause anguished confusion. Two burners are a minimum, three or four ideal.

You have a choice between fuels—alcohol, kerosene, bottled gas, electrical power, or canned heat. Each has its advantages and problems.

Both alcohol and kerosene stoves need a great deal of care and attention in fueling, priming, and starting. Alcohol is cleaner burning but doesn't produce as hot a flame as kerosene and is, therefore, slower cooking. Both require a catch pan for drippings underneath. These two fuels are inexpensive, but kerosene is more readily available wherever boat supplies are sold.

Bottled gas is undiluted and is hotter and faster cooking than gas at home. It emits a mild garlic odor for easy detection of leaks. But don't rely entirely on your nose; check the connections from the tanks to the stove regularly for leaks. Refills of bottled gas are more difficult to come by—they must be ordered from town—so refueling can be a problem.

Canned heat is the safest but also the slowest-cooking fuel. It is available everywhere, and you can stock up and maintain a plentiful supply. No matter which is your prime source of cooking heat, it is a good idea to carry a single-burner solid fuel unit along with your emergency gear. If you have room, take along a hibachi or charcoal grill for a welcome change in your cooking. Hang it over the side of the boat on gimbals, or take it with you to the beach.

Confine your choice to the five . . . don't even look at a gasoline stove. They are highly explosive, and no insurance company will cover the risk.

The manufacturer's manual is your best guide to the maintenance and use of your appliance. If the manual is not at hand, write for a new copy.

✣ STOVE SAFETY

The stove is the greatest hazard on board: Clogged fuel lines, spattered grease, and careless handling of fuel cause most fires at sea. Observe the following safety rules carefully:

- Every cooking area *must* have a fire extinguisher.
- Use the extinguisher on fires caused by oily liquids, grease, or electrical equipment.
- Use water to douse alcohol fires.
- Sprinkle coarse salt to smother small flareups from fat.
- Enclose and smother pan fires with a pot cover.
- Insulate the area around the stove carefully.
- Install your stove on gimbals to keep it level at all times.
- Be sure there is adequate ventilation in the galley area.
- A fixed outside ventilator is standard on many boats, but if your galley doesn't have one, a small portable battery-operated fan affixed to the bulkhead will do the job.
- To dissipate any fumes that may have leaked when the boat has been idle for any length of time, use the fan and open the portholes *before* you use the stove.
- Always turn off the safety valves when the stove is not in use. Leaks are a frequent cause of accidents. To be sure and safe, paint an arrow on the dial with a felt-tipped pen to show the direction for "off." A corresponding mark on the panel below makes for an easy eye check in passing.
- Never fill the storage tanks with liquid fuel while the stove is in use or even warm. Be sure you have enough fuel before you start to cook.
- To avoid spillage, use a funnel to fill the tanks. If you do spill, wipe up every drop!
- When you light any type of stove, *first* strike the match and then turn on the burner. Otherwise an excessive amount of fuel may escape.

KEEP YOUR STOVE CLEAN

- Wipe the stove top daily with vinegar to cut grease buildup.
- Remove burned-on grease with a soap pad while the oven is still warm.
- To rout stubborn grease that won't respond to scrubbing, boil detachable grids in a solution of water and washing soda. Use two tablespoons of soda to a quart of water and boil for 20 minutes.

HOARD WATER

We never fully appreciate how dependent we are on fresh water until the cruising season starts. Everybody thinks of conserving drinking water, but the kids and guests forget that the water supply has to stretch for dishwashing, cooking, cleanup, and personal needs. It's *you* who have to take a 24-hour watch at the taps.

- Watch for drippy faucets and pumps and keep a good supply of rubber washers handy for immediate repairs.
- Fill your tanks at *every* overnight or fueling stop.
- When washing dishes, fill the pan or sink halfway with water and a low-sudsing detergent. After the wash, drain and refill halfway again for the rinse.
- To soften cooked-on foods, soak really dirty pans for at least an hour.
- Use foil to line pans and broilers whenever possible. After cooking peel it off and throw it away.
- Try a little lemon juice and water to soak out and cut grease.
- To get grease off a really burned pan, soak a paper towel in ammonia and cover the burned surface. Tie this into a plastic bag and leave it until morning. A swish of water will finish the job.

 PERSONAL WATER TIPS

The galley isn't the only place that drinks up precious water. The head claims its share, but there are ways to cut waste.

- If water is brought aboard in portable containers, keep the cooking supply separate. That relieves you of one worry when you hear water gurgling.
- During washup, turn on the water just to moisten hands or toothbrush, turn off the tap while you scrub. Turn it on again for the rinse.
- Show children and guests the proper way to use water aboard a boat and caution them often.
- Use premoistened towelettes for freshening up.

EQUIPPING
YOUR GALLEY

The galley is scrubbed and shining, the equipment is in good working order, and you've done a clever job of adding to the storage space. Now it's time to bring aboard all your favorite kitchen utensils.

At home you can afford the luxury of a great array of pots and pans; on board you need utensils that do more than one job. And leave your trusty but dented old castoffs at home; they will be unsteady on a rocky stove and are quicker to rust when exposed to sea air.

For a gold mine of space-saving equipment, prowl around a camping supply store. They carry all sorts of handy little gadgets that save room: nested pots and pans with clamp-on lids, pots with dividers in which to cook two dishes at once, and collapsible colanders and measuring cups. Camping utensils are made of heavy-gauge metal and are less likely to dent and rust. Check them out.

POTS AND PANS

For less work in the galley, invest in attractively decorated pots and pans that double for cooking and serving. Also consider nonstick, coated cookware that needs no special maintenance and washes out with a swish of water. They all have advantages, so pick the utensils that fit your galley style best.

You will want pots and pans deep enough so that food won't slosh over the sides. Remember, too, that no respectable galley pot should be seen without its lid: You can't watch every pot all the time. Your basic lists for pots and pans should include:

- two frying pans, small and large, with lids
- double boiler for six different jobs: as individual pots, as hotplates to keep food warm, to steam leftovers, to heat two dishes at once (top and bottom), to finish a casserole, and to use the hot water in the bottom part to make coffee or tea or for washup water
- large pot with lid for stews, casseroles, and soups
- coffee pot
- tea kettle (much safer than boiling water in an open pan)
- toast rack that fits over a burner

Optional Items

- cake or loaf pan
- folding oven that fits on top of the burners
- muffin or cupcake tin
- pressure cooker
- electric frying pan
- griddles
- disposable foil broiling pans

 BASIC UTENSILS

ice pick
spatula
can openers (two or more)
measuring cups
mixing spoons
cooking forks
measuring spoons
cutting knives
paring knife
juice containers (for storing milk from leaky cartons and leftover soups and stews)
funnel
ladle
knife sharpener
chopper
carrot and potato peeler
colander
juicer
cutting board (sized to fit over the top of the sink)
plastic bowls and jars with tops
pot holders
nested mixing bowls
moisture-proof container for matches

Optional Utensils

corkscrew
egg slicer
tongs
clam shucker
blender

 DISHES AND TABLEWARE

Dishes and tableware are headed for rugged wear, but with today's variety of materials and design, they can be attractive as well as sturdy.

Plastic dishes and stainless steel place settings are the most popular tableware. Metal, enamel baked on metal, and stoneware are distinctive and equally serviceable, so take your pick. Mugs with handles, to be hung on hooks, are more practical then plastic glassware; use them for soups as well as hot and cold beverages.

You may never use paper plates and cups at home, but on

board, where informality is the rule, they are the answer to galley chores. Storage space and disposal room are the only drawbacks when stocking an adequate amount for the whole family on a long cruise. Your best bet is to mix them up —use paper for breakfast and lunch and dishes for dinner. For entertaining, paper is tops and, when set in wicker or plastic holders, is both decorative and sturdy.

Paper Goods to Stock

plates	place mats
cups	toilet tissue
paper towels	plastic and aluminum
garbage bags and ties	wraps
napkins	

⚙ CLEANING SUPPLIES

A ship-shape galley is spanking clean. Be prepared with:

soap powders	glass spray or ammonia
liquid cleaners and deter-	sponges
gents	mop
low-sudsing dishwashing	broom and dustpan
liquid	washing soda and baking
soap pads	soda

⚙ KEEPING THE GALLEY NEAT

Once the paraphernalia is all aboard and stowed, keep your galley neat and tidy. Utensils belong in the cubbies or on their hooks, not on the counter top, ready to crash to the floor with every passing wave. Unlike your kitchen at home, the galley is always on display . . . a working and living part of the boat. Like the deck, keep it cleared for action.

STOCKING AND RUNNING YOUR GALLEY

When men gather to talk about the rugged life of the sea, one hardy salt is bound to hold forth on the simple pleasures of a can of beans and cold beer at the end of a long day's run. Just don't try it on *your* husband! If you want to keep the crew happy, better plan on stocking a good supply of dependable family favorites.

But that doesn't mean you have to spend half your cruising time in the galley. You belong on deck and there are many shortcuts to get you up and out.

PLAN AHEAD

Lists are all-important to a boat mate, but the galley list has top priority. Jot down every item as it needs to be replaced and take the list with you *every* time you go ashore. Stock up as you go . . . it's so much less to bring from home the next time out!

- Plan for, and have on hand, food for three meals a day for every day on board. Travel plans change, and the expected dinner out may be "out" on deck.
- Carry emergency rations. Wind and weather may delay your return, and that means unexpected meals to prepare.
- Plan for in-between snacks, too. Cookies, cheeses, carrot and celery sticks, and hard-boiled eggs stay hunger pangs.
- If you have the stowage room, take along a folding shopping cart. It's amazing how far from the boat those handy little stores are when you're carrying heavy loads.
- Don't depend on picking up a steak in an unknown port. You may arrive after the shops close or find that there is none nearby.
- Every family has its own favorite dishes; the lists in this chapter are only guidelines. Regarding quantity, remember that even picky eaters will be ravenous, so be prepared for anything!

STOCKING THE GALLEY

Pervasive moisture presents a problem in storing both dry and canned goods. Damp air spoils dry things and turns the labels on the cans into drop-offs. Use coffee tins or plastic bags and storage containers to keep staples fresh and label the containers with marking pens.

Dry Goods

coffee	beans
tea	pancake mix
flour	cereals
sugar	instant potatoes
cookies	rice
crackers	spaghetti
biscuit mix	noodles
bread	prepared rices
powdered milk	prepared noodle dishes
matches	dry soups

Canned Goods

canned meats	fruits
sauces (gravy and tomato)	breads
potatoes	soups
juices	tuna fish
baked beans	salmon
vegetables	evaporated milk
party fixings	chili
tomatoes	sausages

Condiments

ketchup	peanut butter
mustard	olives
salt and pepper	vinegar
pickles	maple syrup
spices	jellies
cooking oils	

Dehydrated Foods

Several brands of dehydrated foods are stocked in boating and camping shops. Some packaged meals run from soup to coffee; others contain single servings of everything from fried eggs on up to fancy omelets. Either way, you just add water and heat. The packets are easy to store, excellent for a quick shortcut meal, and a great addition to the galley.

On Ice

Unless you have an efficient cooling unit, go easy on the perishables; they spoil quickly at sea. A few you may want to include:

cheese	salad
bacon	fruits
milk	eggs
fresh sausage	sandwich meats
meats	lemons and limes

Even without a freezer aboard you can still make use of frozen foods. Your cooling unit or a good Styrofoam ice chest will keep frozen food cool enough to defrost slowly over a two- or three-day period. Use the frozen foods the first few days out. Whenever you cook a family favorite at home, keep the ice chest in mind and double the recipe and freeze half for the boat.

PRECOOK AT HOME

If the airlines can prepare meals before departure, why shouldn't you? The dishes that come from home require very little preparation aboard and, because cooked foods last longer under refrigeration than fresh supplies, you can have fast, easy dinners the second or third evening out.

- Prepare the first day's lunch sandwiches at home.
- Premix and form hamburger patties to save time and mess.
- Bring the old picnic standby, fried chicken, to serve hot or cold.
- Stews, casseroles, and spaghetti sauce always taste better a day or two after cooking; so prepare them at home.
- For a long weekend, precook a roast up to the last half hour and then finish it aboard. In no time you'll have dinner *plus* leftovers for sandwiches or hash.

GOURMET TRICKS

Let your imagination take over in the galley. You don't have unlimited space, supplies, or equipment; so cut corners wherever you can. Use prepared mixes, canned and fresh foods, and spices that complement each other to create gourmet menus. Try mixing and matching your canned goods to turn out exciting meals.

- Add an undiluted can of creamed soup (chicken, celery, or mushroom) and drained stewed tomatoes to canned turkey, chicken, shrimp, or tuna and serve on toast or rice.
- Round out a fresh catch of fish or clams with canned shrimp, crabmeat, or clams. Add a can of peas and cream soup and serve on a bed of rice cooked with a bouillon cube or curry powder.
- If the clam catch is scanty, steam them open, chop up the clams, and add them, with the broth, to a can of condensed chowder or vichyssoise.
- Spice up canned string beans with drained stewed tomatoes and a touch of garlic.
- Open a can of sliced tomatoes, add chopped onion, salt, and pepper and pan fry in butter or wrap in aluminum foil for the grill.
- Season a couple of cans of baked beans with a little mustard and ketchup, add canned or fresh frankfurters, and place slices of fresh or canned bacon across the top for extra flavor. Bake and serve with:
- A tangy cold salad—drain one can each of corn and kidney beans, add a little chopped onion and green pepper, and toss with your favorite oil and vinegar dressing.
- Try canned tomato soup and grated cheddar cheese for an instant tomato rarebit on toast.

COOKING UNDER WAY

A galley is just another kitchen . . . until the boat is under way. Then it can become a battlefield with you in uneven contest with the sea. When nothing around you stays in place:

- Plan simple meals for dusty trips. This is the time for dehydrated foods, a casserole in the oven (with the door tightly latched), or heating a one-dish combination of canned goods.

- Put loose articles in the sink or in a dishpan on the floor.
- Use towel racks with suction cups on the ends as movable countertop guard rails.
- Place damp cloths under bowls to hold them steady on a slippery countertop.
- Keep your eye on your pots so your dinner stays on the stove.
- Above all, watch the flame. A gust of wind can blow it out.
- When serving dinner in rocky weather, it may be easier to eat from a plate on your lap rather than on a table.
- Plastic or paper plates that are divided into three sections are the best insurance against individual servings sloshing together into one unappetizing mess.

GALLEY NOTES

- When heating canned goods, remove the top of the can and set it—or two or three—in a pan of water on the stove to heat. Each can serves as its own pot, and there's no pan to wash when the food is hot. You can use the clean water for coffee or for washup.
- Save dishes by letting the crew eat their breakfast cereal out of the individual boxes. The wax-paper linings are sturdy enough to hold milk and sugar.
- If the burners are busy, cook the bacon in the oven for even crispness.
- Attach your can opener to the bulkhead with a long piece of string. Other openers may disappear topside, but you'll always have one at hand.
- Save extra steps when setting the table or cleaning up by stocking an all-purpose plastic pan. Fill it with condiments, flatware, napkins, and glassware and make only one trip to the table or deck.

Aluminum Foil to Speed Galley Chores

- Double wrap loaves of bread and rolls in foil so they stay fresh.
- Keep salad greens crisp in foil in the cooler.
- Cover your countertop or cutting board with foil. When you finish preparations, just whisk the mess away.

 ## TRASH DISPOSAL

Now that you've drained all the cans and eaten all the goodies, you are faced with an ever-growing collection of trash! You can't toss it out to sea, but how do you find the room to keep it until you reach port?

- Open both ends of cans and stamp them flat. It's amazing how small they really are.
- Do the same for boxes.
- Nest empty jars and save one or two, with screwtops, for runny, messy wastes.
- Stock up on plastic waterproof garbage bags and the giant-size trash bags. Seal them tight with rubber bands or twists.

GETTING IT ALL TOGETHER

PLANNING YOUR CRUISES

There's a lot more to cruising than just hopping aboard and casting off the lines. A successful boating season depends on a good deal of planning. Even the organization of a day's sail is complicated with dozens of details. There are easy ways to keep it all in order:

 ## KEEP YOUR LISTS TO KEEP YOUR COOL

- Keep the boat in perfect condition and see to all repairs as they are needed.
- Keep running lists of the food, linen, clothing, and recreational equipment you need on board for all occasions. Have your boat supplies up to date.
- Shop and try to take the supplies and gear to the boat well in advance of departure.
- Between trips, keep a "boat box" in a convenient spot at home. It's the easy way to collect clean laundry and odds and ends.

PLAN AHEAD FOR WEEKENDS AND EXTENDED CRUISES

- Plan the *kind* of trip you most enjoy—quiet gunkholes, busy marinas, or sightseeing.
- Be realistic. Pick a destination well within the speed and cruising range of the boat. Pushing to reach a too-distant port may well take the flavor from the trip.
- Allow plenty of time for the unexpected: storms, mechanical difficulty, winds. And—who knows—you may find a perfect spot on the way and linger a while.
- During the height of the season call the marina well in advance to reserve an overnight berth.
- Check your charts and plan food and fuel stops. Also note the location of emergency harbors along the route.
- Limit the day's run. Even old salts find a six- or eight-hour stretch wearing.

CRUISING GUIDES

Many state and national park recreational agencies, gasoline companies, and boating magazines offer free cruising guides for areas all over the country to help you plan interesting trips. These are worthwhile to check out for information about your own area, too. There may be spots you have never explored. The guides make absorbing reading during the long winter months, and when the boating season comes around you can have your vacation all charted out. So take advantage of a good thing and . . . happy cruising!

CHILDREN ABOARD

Boating is a family affair, and that means kids. Just remember that youngsters can kick up as much trouble on board as at home. But at sea nonsense can be dangerous; safety must be your first concern and discipline the order of the day. Once children realize that what passes at home will not be tolerated on the boat, everyone will be much happier and safer.

Children feel comfortable with a clear line of authority, but too rigid an approach can be just as bad as an abandoned crew. So put the rules in a fun way by playing the Navy game. As admiral, you insist on a tight ship, always on the alert, with each person responsible for his own job. A slow response is as bad as none, and mutiny is the cardinal sin. Make sure your rules are also clearly understood by the parents of visiting children. Otherwise their thoughtlessness might incite your offspring to riot!

⚓ TEACHING SAFETY

Children may not fully understand the words "danger" and "drowning." If they do, they can become frightened and reject boating entirely. The soundest approach stresses the fun of boating and underplays the danger. Point out that there are safety rules at sea just as there are at home for bike riding and crossing the street.

Boating safety for children depends on careful attention to the rules for life preservers, to routine procedures on board, and to swimming precautions. Alert parental eyes prevent antics from becoming accidents.

⚓ LIFE PRESERVERS

The American Red Cross manual calls for every person, adult and child, to wear a life preserver at all times aboard a boat. This rule must be strictly observed on runabouts and small sailboats. Sudden swells are hazardous to all small craft, and under sail there is the added danger of a swinging boom or heeling over in a strong wind.

In practice many adults don't wear preservers and children are quick to try to imitate. But they should not be allowed this freedom until they can pass a stiff swimming test, perhaps a 100-yard swim with rest stops. Make the distinction between parental privilege and youngster's ability. Take the simple approach of explaining that when he can swim well enough to take care of himself should he fall overboard, he may go without the preserver. It's also a good incentive to learn to swim well!

Preserver Precautions

- Buy only Coast Guard approved preservers.
- The type of preserver that holds the head above the water is safer than the ring that fits around the waist.

- To fit snugly preservers must be correctly sized for the wearer. Sizes are clearly marked on the label.
- Tie the preserver securely and double check later to see that it hasn't worked loose. Untied straps can entangle a child in the water, fail to hold up his head, or simply allow the preserver to float away.
- Keep the preservers in the car and put them on each child as he gets out. Some children are capable of landing in the drink from the dock or tender before they even see the boat!

SAFETY PROCEDURES ON BOARD

Tell children clearly and specifically what is expected:

- The first rule on any boat—listen for the skipper's commands and obey promptly.
- The second rule on a sailboat—listen for "mind the boom" and "coming about" warnings and duck your head promptly.
- Children who are not asked to assist in docking, anchoring, or departure from the dock must sit down and stay down during those maneuvers.
- Children are not allowed to wander on the deck or dock. Specify the off-limit areas.
- Warn children not to walk or move around unnecessarily. Show them how to change places while holding onto a rail, gunwhale, or back of a seat.
- Establish a routine of safety drills. Make a game of it if you wish, but practice until your brood can be counted on to respond on the double to "man overboard," "fire," and "abandon ship" alarms (see p. 114).

SWIMMING RULES

- Anchor the boat securely before allowing anyone in the water.

- Attach a life ring to a line and float it in the water as a rest stop for a tired swimmer and as a boundary marker for the swimming area. Caution that there is to be no swimming beyond the ring without permission.
- Set up a "buddy" system that makes each swimmer responsible for his partner at all times.
- An adult must be stationed as the on-deck life guard while children are in the water.

☸ JOBS FOR JUNIORS

Boat chores give children a sense of participation and responsibility. They pitch in willingly and have pride in their boat when the whole family works together. Take advantage of their natural enthusiasm with jobs that keep them out of mischief and contribute to *your* leisure.

Deck jobs a child can handle include polishing chrome, washing windows, coiling and stowing lines, and helping with the washdown. Below decks the chores are basically the same as at home; washing and drying dishes, setting the table, and making up bunks.

Insist that chores be done right away, not later. And make it a hard and fast rule that no one leaves the boat until every assigned job is completed, lines are coiled, and hose is stowed.

☸ KEEP THE CHILDREN BUSY

Boating naturally appeals to the imagination of children. Even a broken-down rowboat set in the middle of a playground will keep them playing happily for hours. But the novelty soon wears off. Don't plan long runs every day. If you must put in a long day, try to stop for lunch and a swim.

Children need games and amusements to keep them from

becoming bored and driving you crazy. Try to stay a step or two ahead with imaginative boat games.

On Deck

- Appoint one child as the "lookout" and give him an inexpensive pair of binoculars to help the skipper spot landmarks and buoys.
- Give out small compasses with which the children can follow the chart and keep the course.
- Teach the kids to make sailors' knots; they'll be busy practicing for hours (see p. 105).
- Point out the different types of boats and keep score on how many they name correctly.
- An inexpensive camera not only holds a child's interest but also helps keep his boating memories alive for years.

Below Deck

- Encourage children to watch quietly as the skipper charts his course.
- Keep one cubby or ditty bag just for the kids' games. Let them color, play scrabble or cards, and make cutouts with a pair of blunt scissors.
- Suggest art projects with boating themes; boats, sea, and harbor scenes.
- With airplane glue, the children can paste their shell collections into interesting objects, on boxes to make decorative gifts or onto paper as attractive collages.
- Encourage them to keep a log or a scrapbook as reference for the inevitable "my vacation" school composition.

In the Water

- Organize in-the-water volleyball and basketball games. Equipment is available on floating Styrofoam mountings and can be assembled in minutes from a few stowable parts.

- Use inflatable mattresses and Styrofoam boards for extra fun and safety.
- If you have a dinghy, your problems are over forever. Once the children learn to handle it properly and pass their safety tests, they'll be busy for hours and you'll never have to run another errand.

GOOD BOATING MANNERS

You love your kids, but be sure everyone else enjoys them by impressing them with the importance of good boating manners. Even a toddler can follow these few simple rules:

- Never board another boat without permission.
- Do not peek in portholes.
- Never track dirt and/or sand aboard.
- Do not shout or run on the dock.
- Respect the property of others. Never touch anything that does not belong to you.
- *Never* touch the lines or fenders on any boat, including your own.
- Don't even *sit* in someone else's dinghy without permission.
- To be welcome on all docks, always be courteous and helpful. Offer to catch lines, attach hoses, and watch out for younger children.

BOATING WITH BABY

At sea, as on land, a baby is a lot easier to watch than a toddler or an older child. At least babies stay put. However, there are special steps to take for the seagoing infant.

- Stock disposable diapers and extra plastic garbage bags with twists to seal them tightly until you find a trash can ashore.

- If you run out of disposables, rinse dirty diapers overboard in a net bag to remove most of the odor until you get to a washing machine. Be sure to equip your diaper can or bag with a tight cover or seal and an effective deodorant.
- Fill a thermos with boiling water before you go to bed. It will stay hot enough to warm that 2:00 A.M. bottle and save sleepy fumbling at the galley stove.
- If there's no room for a small playpen, the next best thing is a babygate attached to the outside of a bunk.
- Pad the sides of any play area with a soft quilt or blanket.
- A hat and lightweight cover-up clothes will protect the baby's delicate skin against the hot sun when he's out on deck.
- Rig a *babytender* for the infant just beginning to walk. Run an overhead wire fore and aft through the cabins and out on deck. Attach one end of a line to the wire with a snap fastener and the other end to junior's life vest. Give him enough slack to kneel and let him go. The vest will cushion falls.
- Or you can attach a walking harness, with enough slack for movement, right to the boat.
- Sew little bells to the straps of a toddler's preserver to keep you posted on his whereabouts.
- Attach a steering wheel, such as the kind used in cars, to the bulkhead to keep a little one busy and happy.

⛭ THE REWARDS OF BOATING

Boating teaches children self-reliance in ways that cannot be matched ashore; courtesy and concern for others, respect for property, and obedience to rules are permanent lessons. Caution follows knowledge, and independence comes with experience. Like all sailors children feel the fulfillment of contact with the sea and a strong sense of adventure that lasts all their lives.

GUESTS ABOARD

CHAPTER 10

Of course you will want to share your favorite sport with your landlubber friends, but, before you get carried away and start issuing invitations, give a second (and third) thought to the care and feeding of boating guests.

Most people are delighted with a "yachting" invitation and make enthusiastic guests. But not every couple who are great shore companions wear well in confined quarters over a long period. Don't invite the friend who hates the water and gets seasick at the *thought* of a boat . . . you'll never convince her that boating is fun. So choose carefully; you'll be glad you did.

TRIP PLANNING

After you have decided whom to honor with the first invitation of the season, design the trip with *them* in mind.

- Don't feel compelled to invite friends for a whole weekend. A day of swimming, fishing, and picnicking can be just as pleasant as a long trip.
- Limit your guests to the number the boat can comfortably accommodate and *you* can serve.
- As an alternative to crowded sleeping accommodations aboard, head for a marina with a nearby hotel or motel. Your guests will be more comfortable ashore, and you can spend your days together on the water.
- For active, restless souls, plan a stop at a busy port with many facilities. Give the quiet ones a peaceful anchorage, an evening of talk, and an early bedtime.

⚓ BRIEF GUESTS BEFOREHAND

Once you settle on a trip plan, let your guests know what to expect. Start them off right.

- Warn them that the weather determines whether or not you sail that day. A doubtful forecast courts misery with everyone huddled in a small, heaving cabin.
- Changing weather and winds may cause delays. Prepare them for the possibility of a late return.
- Suggest the proper clothing for your destination.
- Give them guidelines on packing (ditty bag or duffel) and keeping clothing to a minimum.
- You love your boat, but it's no cruise ship. So prepare them for the limitations on board. If you have no shower, they will need robes for the trek to marina facilities.
- Be firm about proper boating shoes that will not mar your beautiful decks.
- Check any diet restrictions or preferences your guests may have.
- Remind them that time and tide wait for no man, and a prompt arrival at the dock will be greatly appreciated.

 WELCOME ABOARD

Everyone needs guidance in unfamiliar surroundings; don't be bashful about explaining how you want things done. As soon as your guests arrive and the gear is stowed, give them a guided tour.

On Deck

- Point out the location of the fire extinguishers and life jackets and show them how they work.
- Ask them to obey the skipper's directions immediately and ask why later.
- Remind them to be extremely cautious with cigarettes and ashes.
- Your long hours with paint and varnish brushes will be for naught if you don't *order* them to watch the brightwork.
- A word of caution: If the going gets rough, everyone must sit down and stay down.
- Assure your guests they will be most helpful during docking and anchoring procedures by sitting down and staying out of the way unless given a specific job.
- Let the captain give the word that no one is to touch the charts or binoculars unless asked to help. The electrical equipment (radio, direction finder, etc.) are adjusted to the captain's needs.

Below Deck

- As all the signs say, there are no plumbers at sea, so explain the operation of the head and what should *not* go into it.
- Remind all that head facilities are limited. The water and towel supplies should be carefully hoarded.
- Inspection of the galley is in order to point out the location of (and a word of caution for) the ice chest and soft drink stores. Be pleasant and firm if you don't want help in the galley.

PUT EVERYONE TO WORK

Even a fabulous hostess can't do everything—help the skipper, cook, clean—and still have time to entertain. Let your guests pitch in. Some jobs for a new hand include: making bunks, dusting up, cleaning the head, serving drinks, and taking over the galley for the cocktail hour. Divide up the chores in advance and you'll all have more time for fun.

 ## THE COCKTAIL HOUR

A few landlubbers have the notion that a cruise is a good excuse for drinking. Not while you are under way it isn't! Some skippers even refuse to allow alcoholic beverages to be served until the boat is in port. How, or whether, you convey this to your guests is your concern, but—a word to the wise—boating accidents have been caused by one too many even when tied up at the dock!

Part of the fun of boating is the easy camaraderie of the people you meet and the spontaneity of parties. When the mob descends on you, be prepared with snacks that don't drip all over the deck. A half dozen pairs of feet sloshing through fallen canapes (and they fall more easily even on a gently rocking boat) make a horrible mess, and *you* have to clean it up.

For Neat Nibbling

carrot sticks
curls of green pepper and celery
cheeses
hard-boiled eggs (roll them in black pepper for spice)
pitted olives
dry-roasted nuts
pickled mushrooms on toothpicks
chunks of salami or bologna

tiny cocktail sausages or meat balls heated (then drained)
pates
spreads that don't drip

Don't serve drippy dips or greasy chips. Save your decks from anything preserved in oil.

⚓ GUEST INSURANCE

If these warnings seem a bit overwhelming, think of them as guest insurance. For great fun—be careful in your choice.

PICNICKING AND BEACH PARTIES

Who said a picnic is a delightful, impromptu affair? Try it. Throw a few things together at the last minute, and when you get the whole tribe to shore you'll discover all the important items you forgot.

If you really want a happy, trouble-free picnic, organize it in advance with prepacked picnic and ready bags. When the next inviting island or beach comes into cruising range, you'll be packed and ready to go in a few minutes.

CUSTOMIZED PICNIC BASKET

A good picnic basket can be expensive to buy, but they are very simple to make. Choose an inexpensive but sturdy wicker basket of the size that suits your needs and fits your storage locker. Add to its capacity by sewing or stapling varying lengths of elastic loops on the lid with heavy thread. They will hold eating and serving utensils and paper plates, cups, and napkins.

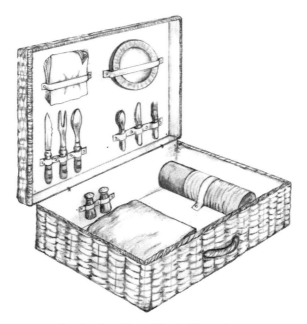

Customize Your Picnic Basket

Next cut out a thin piece of plywood to fit snugly half-way down in the basket. If any form of carpentry frightens you, have a lumberyard measure and cut the wood. Now you can place your heavier things on the bottom, put your divider in the middle and have a firm base for lighter items on top. When you've unpacked on shore, the divider becomes a tray for the salt and pepper and other small items that mysteriously disappear in the sand.

Into the Picnic Basket

- paper plates, cups, and napkins
- knives, forks, and spoons
- serving utensils
- at least one cutting knife
- clam opener
- thermos for hot and cold drinks

- can and bottle openers, attached with string
- garbage bags and twists for cleanup
- salt and pepper
- sugar packets
- individual packets of ketchup, mustard, and jams
- premoistened towelettes
- aluminum foil (fold it two or three times and shape to form efficient and disposable pans for the grill or to wrap corn and potatoes for the fire)

If someone in your crew is handy with a rod, include a fish knife and board. Also add the extras that you fancy—that's part of the customizing.

 ## THE CHILDREN'S READY BAG

Picnics are times for fun as well as food, so don't forget to provide for the small fry. The best preparation is a special bag permanently packed with their personal beach supplies. Buy a tote bag or make one out of sailcloth by folding the cloth in half, seaming two sides and using the open side as a drawstring closing. For a deluxe model, line it with plastic to preserve the contents against spillage and dunking. Stock each ready bag with all those little things that the child will need on the outing.

- ball, sand toys, pail, and shovel
- coloring book and crayons
- inflatable animal, ball, or raft
- extra swim suit
- plastic bags for collecting treasure
- cookies and candy
- sun hat
- small compass so he can explore
- tissues
- any extras geared to his special interest

 THE ADULT READY BAG

What about your own long, lazy afternoon on the beach? It will be more comfortable if you have your own ready bag always stocked.

- suntan lotion
- sunglasses
- sunshade or beach hat
- swim cap
- tissues
- toilet tissue
- comb or brush
- simple first-aid kit (cotton, antiseptic, and adhesive bandages)
- pocket book or magazines
- extra cigarettes and matches

After each excursion, restock the picnic basket and your ready bags to be sure that they are complete for your next picnic. If you don't have room for a beach umbrella, take two or three sturdy sticks or poles and drape a strip of canvas over them for shade.

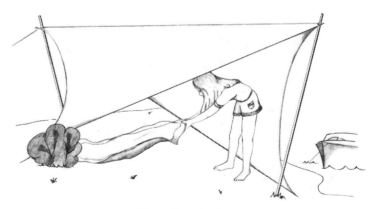

Rig a Sunshade

⚓ BEACHING SAFEGUARDS

If you go ashore by dinghy:

* Avoid muddy or obstructed bottoms; look for a clear, sandy area.
* Secure the dinghy with an anchor or line tied to a tree before unloading supplies.
* Check at intervals to make sure that the dinghy has not drifted.
* To warn the others away from deep spots and dropoff areas, the best swimmer should explore the offshore bottom before allowing anyone in the water.

Safety Precautions For the Kids

* Wear sneakers if going into woods.
* Observe the boundary line for exploring.
* Do not go into the water without adult permission.
* Return all equipment to your ready bag when finished.
* Return to the base instantly when you hear the prearranged signal (a loud blast of a gym whistle, for example).

⚓ A BARBEQUE

Cold picnics are fine, but beach parties can be something special if, like steaks, they have a little sizzle. When you can't face another sandwich, bring ashore a portable grill or simply an oven rack to convert to your own instant barbeque grill.

Build Your Own Barbeque

* Scoop a fire hole in the sand.
* Tamp solidly to build up the edges of the excavation.
* Send out scouts to collect stones for a two-sided support on

which to rest the oven rack. If the hole is deep enough, simply put the rack right over it.

- Fuel the fire in the hole. Charcoal makes the hottest and most reliable flame, but paper, twigs, and dry driftwood burn well after a little coaxing.

KEEP THE DRINKS COLD

- Canned soda is preferable to breakable bottles.
- Place the cans in a heavily weighted net bag at the water's edge to keep them cold.
- For the thermos, frozen drink concentrates are best. The ice chest on the boat will store a wide selection in a small space.

PICNIC FROM THE SEA

Grills are meant for more than hot dogs and hamburgers. For a palate-pleasing change of pace, picnic from the sea with fresh grilled fish (but take a substitute just in case the fish aren't running). To add to the fun—and your menu—organize a clamming expedition.

First catch your clams:
along the webbing edges of saline coves
you'll find the precious wedges.
—Crofut

There's as much truth as poetry there; Crofut knew his clams. They are found in the mud flats of sheltered, shallow bays, in gravel-filled pockets in the rocks on tidal headlands, and in the hard-packed sands of beaches. Watch for the telltale holes in the sand for the water spouts of soft-shelled clams.

⊕ CLAMMING

- Ask the local Chamber of Commerce (or a friendly native) whether you need a clamming license, where the best clam beds are located, and if there is any local pollution.
- Champion clammers swear by their fingers; rubber or plastic kitchen gloves save the manicure. However, to make your own clamming fork or shovel, blunt the tips of an ordinary garden tool with tape.
- For hard-shelled clams, burrow about one to two inches below the sand and probe gently in a four-inch radius. The clams will feel rocklike and are easily pulled to the surface.
- For soft-shelled clams you have to dig down about three to five inches. Dig quickly; when they hear you coming they dig down, too.
- Discard very small clams (or open ones—they're dead); leave them to grow for next year.
- In the excitement of dragging for a bucket of clams it is easy to forget the intensity of the sun. Protect your back and head.
- Dig only what you will eat. Remember that other clammers will be along.
- Rinse the clams by filling and emptying the bucket a few times with salt water.
- Use the clam opener if you enjoy them raw and if there is no pollution. You can also put the unopened hard-shelled clams on the barbeque grill and watch them open in their own juices. It's a taste you will never forget.
- Soft-shelled clams have to be steamed open in a tightly lidded pot with about two cups of water. Allow about 10 minutes' cooking time after the water boils.

Have your clams or fish with vegetables cooked in foil, corn roasted in the fire, warm rolls, and perhaps a salad tossed before you left the boat. Cold fresh fruit tops it all off.

 LEAVING THE PICNIC

Don't cast your picnic leftovers on the waters or leave them to litter the beach. Carry them back to the boat or bury them deep. On your next visit you'll be glad you did.

THE FEMININE LOOK

It's easy to lose yourself in a world of flying foam and cracking sails, but that moment of truth when you finally see yourself in the mirror can be quite a shock. A weathered, salty look, complete with paint-spattered dungarees, may be flattering on a man, but it definitely doesn't do a thing for you!

In spite of drenching salt sprays and lots of sun, you *can* preserve your image. It only needs a sensible beauty care routine and a simple wardrobe.

⚓ BEAUTY CARE

Exercise, sun, and sea air trim away inches and give you a healthy glow that can't be bought in a bottle. You don't need a locker full of beauty preparations to keep you crisp and fresh.

Hair Tips

- Keep your flowing locks tied back and out of the way. Long hair impairs your vision and can tangle in the lines.
- The sun has bleaching power far stronger than any bottled preparation. If you have problem hair, keep it covered.
- Go easy on the hair spray; it gets sticky and gummy in damp air.
- Be sparing in the use of setting lotion as well. Salt air gives hair extra body.
- Try a dry shampoo for a quick freshener.
- If you have room, carry a dryer along for use at the dock.

Pamper Your Skin

- A sea burn is a three-way burn from the sun, wind, and reflected glare off the water; it can be severe. If you have fair skin, keep it covered. Even if you tan beautifully, start the season off with suntan lotion.
- Wear sunglasses to avoid squint lines around your eyes.
- Sun dries the skin, so don't skimp on lotions for your body, face, and hands. Lubricate your skin with a rich lotion to cream away the white, flaky look that appears when your skin gets too dry or your tan fades.

Hand Care

- Long lovely nails have no place on a boat. File them short and neat.
- Before painting or varnishing, rub petroleum jelly into your cuticles to protect them against the drying effects of the turpentine cleanup afterwards.
- A dab of perfume was never meant to cover up fish odors. If you don't have rubber gloves, here's a better way to handle fish: Soak your hands in cold water *before* touching raw fish. After preparing the fish, rub hands with moist salt. Then rinse in hot water. Finally, wash with soap.

⚓ CHOOSING BOAT CLOTHING

For Safety's Sake

- Wear bright colors—red, orange, yellow, or white—so that even in the water you are always clearly visible.
- Save the ruffles and bows for shore. On board they can catch on lines.
- Be sure your clothing fits comfortably but not snugly. You'll forget fashion if your perfectly tailored slacks split at the seams when you bend or reach.

Be Practical

- Capitalize on drip-dry synthetic fabrics.
- Choose double-duty clothes (jackets with zip-in linings and reversible separates).
- Color coordinate separates to create different outfits; for example, a pair of yellow shorts, a pair in blue, and both yellow and blue shirts all interchange into four different outfits. One pair of sneakers, blue or yellow, goes with each combination.
- Look for pockets in jackets, blouses, and pants. You'll need them to hold small items.

What to Keep On Board

The standard daytime wardrobe is a bathing suit or a T-shirt over shorts or dungarees, at night slacks and a blouse. To cover all situations, also stow:

- three shirts, two for daytime and one for an evening change
- an extra pair of slacks to wear to town or on deck at night
- boat shoes—sneakers or nonskid type
- underclothes
- pajamas (Even if you sleep in the buff at home, the lack of privacy on board makes sleepwear a must.)

- cover-up robe required on the dock in many marinas and clubs and handy for the ladies' room shower.
- foul-weather gear (waterproof, not just water repellent, for complete protection and vented for coolness).
- a warm sweater, jacket, or windbreaker (for the crisp evening that follows a hot afternoon).
- an outfit for town (Slacks for ladies and tieless shirts for men are generally acceptable along the water route. But to be safe bring along one evening outfit; a basic drip-dry dress, a pair of shoes, a small bag, and a dressy sweater for yourself and daughter; a pair of slacks, a shirt, a tie, and a jacket for your husband and son. Shoes and clothing not often used should be kept clean and dry in plastic bags and aired periodically.)
- soft folding ditty bags or handbags that stow easily
- snugly fitting hats (for protection against the sun).
- accessories (A bright scarf knotted at the waist, a great belt, or a gaudy neckerchief adds color and variety even to a plain white shirt and blue jeans. There's always locker room for extras.)

PETS ABOARD

Who decides whether your pet puts out to sea? He does, and make no mistake about it. To discover if your pet takes to boating, start him off slowly and proceed with caution.

- Take him to the boat yard just to get acquainted. Give him the run of the boat and let him explore to his heart's content.
- After a couple of visits, turn on the engines to accustom him to the vibrations and sound.
- Next take a quick spin in calm water to familiarize him with the motion.
- Gradually increase the length of the trips until you feel he has gotten his sea legs.

Most pets, particularly young ones, take to sea with enthusiasm. The few who don't probably have a deep-rooted fear of water or a sensitivity to the motion of the boat. If this describes your pet, don't fight it; leave him home. Once your pet decides he likes boating and wants to join the family, there are preparations and precautions just as there are for children.

⚓ GEAR

- heavy-based dishes for water and food
- a blanket or rug scrap for his *bunk*. Even animals need a security blanket!
- his own swimming towel
- grooming articles (brush and comb)
- collar and leash, even for cats
- toys or familiar things from home

⚓ FEEDING

- Cut down on food rations; with less exercise he needs less food.
- Decrease the quantity of water, too. Some dogs love to lick an ice cube for cool refreshment.
- Even an animal who does not get seasick will digest his meal better without the rocking motion of a boat. Feed him after you come to port.
- Do not leave leftover food in the dish. Clear it away immediately. It sours faster in the heat, and there's one in every crowd who steps in the bowl!

⚓ WALKING

- Take pets to grassy areas for their walks. It is discourteous to mess the docks.
- When at anchor, arrangements must be made to take a dog to shore at least twice and preferably three times a day. If he likes the water, you can swim ashore with him or use the dinghy.

- Animals should be taken ashore only on a leash. When loose, they are a hazard to people walking or standing on the dock. A carefree romp may topple someone into the water.
- Even cats should adhere to the above rule. They are curious creatures, and you never know when one will decide to explore. In strange surroundings it is not likely that they will find their way back.
- If possible, retrain the animal to paper. It may come in handy in the middle of the night.

SAFETY

- No animal should be allowed on the bow of the boat. Not only is there danger of his falling overboard, but when the anchor is let out there is the very real danger that he will become fouled in the lines and be drawn overboard. No matter how fast you haul him in, he won't stand a chance.
- When leaving or returning to dock or when going through locks, all animals should be put below deck or leashed to one spot. These procedures are enough without a careening animal underfoot.
- Never force your pet to go swimming. Many dogs have a fear of the water and, contrary to popular belief, not all dogs know how to swim.
- There are round, neck life preservers for animals and they work very well. It's an added precaution if you are nervous about your pet.

COURTESY

- If you go ashore in the evening, check back to see if your pet is howling. He may not know it's inconsiderate to others, but you do!

If you set the scene, your pet can easily adapt to boating and it's nice to take him along.

COURTESY

★

Boating is a cooperative sport, and in the growing group of enthusiasts it is rare to find careless or brusque behavior. At one time or another we all rely on help. There are always willing hands to bring a boat safely to the dock and promptly assist in a tight spot. Smiles and friendly waves to every passing sailor is our acknowledgment of membership in a very special group.

MARINA MANNERS

In communal marina life, noise and dirt are more offensive than at home where you have a measure of privacy. When you're berthed in close quarters, sandwiched in with many other boats with your neighbor only a dock's width away, the golden rule becomes a matter of common sense.

- Never toss garbage overboard. Every yard has conveniently placed cans for waste disposal.
- Keep the noise down at late parties.
- Don't spread your gear haphazardly over the dock. It is unsightly and hazardous.
- Be considerate when you plug into electrical power lines. If you turn on every appliance aboard you may blow the fuses for everyone.
- Never set foot on another boat without permission. Always ask, "May I come aboard?"
- Many marinas and yacht clubs do not permit the use of a marine head in the harbor. Observe all regulations.
- Courtesy visiting privileges in the use of facilities is reciprocal among yacht clubs. Know the rules and observe them when you visit.

⚓ IN THE BOAT YARD

- Come prepared with all the tools you will need to work on your boat. Most yards will not lend their tools, and it is an imposition to interrupt other owners to borrow theirs.
- If you are stymied and must borrow, return the articles promptly and in good condition.
- Never touch equipment in the yard or on the deck of another boat without permission.
- Check before you start a dirty job. Don't let your dust settle on another boat's new coat of varnish or paint.
- Always clean up your mess. Leave the area as clean as when you started.

⚓ UNDER WAY

- Slow down when passing through an anchorage or overtaking slower boats. Don't set them awash.
- Observe the speed limits in harbors. Harbor police give tickets, too.

- Stay clear of races. If you must go through, change course in order to pass as far astern of the other boats as possible.
- Keep your conversations short on the ship-to-shore phone. There are few channels and many callers.

⚙ DOCKING

- When tying up to a temporary dock, leave enough room for other boats.
- If the dock has room for only one boat, be prompt with fueling, phoning, or taking on water. Move out again as soon as possible; other boats may be waiting.
- Keep your lines clear when casting off so that they won't foul another boat.
- In order to cast off it is sometimes necessary to remove the lines of another boat that are on the same pole or cleat. Be careful to replace them correctly and securely.

KEEPING IT ALL
TOGETHER

BOATSMANSHIP

State laws require licenses before anyone may drive a car, but for some unfathomable reason no such safeguards apply to boats . . . anybody can buy one and take off! Nautical licensing is in the discussion stage, but, until it passes into law, ignorance of existing maritime statutes is no excuse. Violations will get you into trouble with the Coast Guard and harbor police. So bone up on the rules to stay on the right side of the law and, more important, to keep your family safe.

Although it is the skipper's responsibility to know and observe the rules of the road, you must know the basics when you spell him at the wheel. Join one of the excellent seamanship courses offered by the United States Coast Guard or the Power Squadron. Or pick up what you need by reading and following the skipper's lead.

There are many excellent books devoted solely to seamanship, and it is not our intent to offer a short-cut course. Rather we have outlined briefly, for quick reference, the chief points that come up most often.

RULES OF THE ROAD

There are no traffic lights or full stop signs on the water. To prevent collisions one boat must have the acknowledged right of way. The rules of the road are regulations designed to avoid such accidents. The federal government publishes three separate sets of rules: for western rivers, for the Great Lakes, and for inland areas. These vary slightly so be sure to get the set that applies to your region and any section that you may visit.

 WHISTLE SIGNALS

Power boats communicate by prescribed whistle signals. Failure to give or comprehend proper signals is the most common cause of collision.

A whistle signal is always answered with an identical signal to show the maneuver is understood. However, if the meaning is not clear or the answering boat sees danger, then he replies with four short blasts. Both boats immediately stop or reverse engines until, through an exchange of signals, understanding is reached.

The Meaning of the Signals

1 long blast. Warning to unseen boats; given when backing out of a blind slip or approaching a bend in a river or channel where other boats may be hidden

1 short blast. I am going to starboard

2 short blasts. I am going to port

3 short blasts. I am reversing engines

4 short blasts. I do not understand, cannot be done, danger

Fog signals vary in the three sets of rules, but in all three they must be given at regular prescribed intervals of not more than one minute apart.

THE RIGHT OF WAY FOR POWER BOATS

The boat with the acknowledged right-of-way is known as *privileged* and is entitled to hold its course and speed until safely clear of any other vessel. The other boat, which must give way, is called *burdened* and must take action to prevent collision.

The three most common situations for power boats are: meeting head-on, overtaking another boat, and crossing. The rules that govern these maneuvers are shown in the diagrams below.

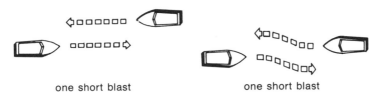

one short blast   one short blast

Passing in Head-On Situations: When boats approach each other from opposite or nearly opposite directions, each alters course to pass port-to-port after the proper whistle signals have been exchanged.

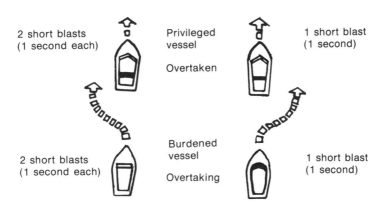

2 short blasts (1 second each)   Privileged vessel   1 short blast (1 second)

Overtaken

2 short blasts (1 second each)   Burdened vessel   1 short blast (1 second)

Overtaking

Overtaking Situations: The overtaking vessel is burdened and must signal the privileged boat as to the side on which he will pass. He must wait until the signal has been returned before passing.

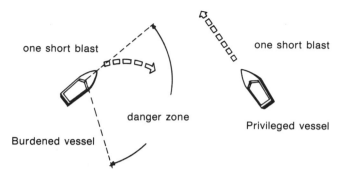

one short blast

one short blast

danger zone

Privileged vessel

Burdened vessel

Crossing Situations: When two boats cross so as to involve the risk of collision, the vessel which has the other on her starboard (in the danger zone) is burdened and must give way by slowing down and passing astern.

THE RIGHT OF WAY FOR SAILBOATS

- Sailboats under sail have the right-of-way over power boats at all times except when they are overtaking. Then the sailboat must stay clear.
- Sailboats moving under combined sail and power must conform to the rules for power boats.
- The right-of-way between two sailboats is determined by the direction of the wind in reference to their sailing direction.
- As a general rule the privileged boat is on the starboard tack, the burdened boat on the port.
- A sailboat running free (before the wind) is burdened and must stay clear of a close-hauled boat, which is sailing as close to the wind as possible.
- When both boats are running free with the wind, the leeward boat (downwind) is privileged over the windward (upwind) in order not to cut off the wind from the leeward boat.

LIGHTS

From sunset to sunrise, under way or at anchor, every boat must carry proper lights. They are instant identification to help you spot moving vessels and to maneuver your own boat in relation to the other's position. The rules for lights vary according to the size and class of the vessel, for pleasure boats, and for commercial vessels. These running lights must be shown by all engine-propelled boats under way at night:

Green light.   starboard
Red light.   port
White lights.   stern and bow
High white light.   mast light on a sailboat under power
All boats must also show a white light when at anchor.

Interpreting Lights

- Green and white lights means that you are approaching a powered boat from starboard.
- A red light and a high white one means you are approaching a sailboat under power on the port side.
- When you see only a red or a green light, you are approaching a sailboat under sail.
- Red and green lights with a white light at the same level or slightly higher signifies that you are approaching a powered boat head on.
- One required white light shows a boat at anchor.

⚓ THE BUOYAGE SYSTEM

The United States Coast Guard (and in some instances the United States Corps of Engineers) maintain buoys and markers on all navigable waterways and prescribed off-shore limits. In addition to the lateral buoyage system, which includes channel markers, there are buoys with lights to assist night pilots, markers to indicate rocks and obstructions, and buoys with bells to aid navigation in fog. The diagram opposite shows the major sea signs and markers.

- When entering a channel, the red, even-numbered *nuns,* are

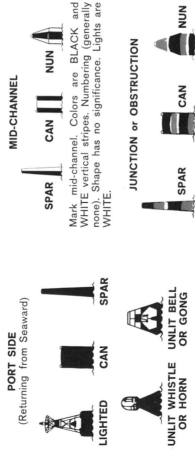

STARBOARD SIDE
(Returning from Seaward)

SPAR   NUN   LIGHTED

UNLIT BELL
OR GONG   UNLIT WHISTLE
OR HORN

Mark starboard side of channel and obstructions. Color is RED. Numbers are EVEN. Shape is NUN (spar, sound and light buoys have no shape significance). Lights are RED or WHITE.

MID-CHANNEL

SPAR   CAN   NUN

Mark mid-channel. Colors are BLACK and WHITE vertical stripes. Numbering (generally none). Shape has no significance. Lights are WHITE.

JUNCTION or OBSTRUCTION

SPAR   CAN   NUN

Mark junction or obstruction. Pass on either side. Preferred channel is indicated by color of top band. Colors are RED and BLACK. Horizontal bands. Numbering (generally none). Shape is CAN or NUN, based on color of top band. Also other shapes. Lights RED, WHITE, or GREEN.

PORT SIDE
(Returning from Seaward)

LIGHTED   CAN   SPAR

UNLIT WHISTLE
OR HORN   UNLIT BELL
OR GONG

Mark port side of channel and obstructions. Color is BLACK. Numbers are ODD. Shape is CAN (spar, sound and light buoys have no shape significance). Lights are GREEN or WHITE.

kept to starboard. Remember this by the words "red, right, returning."

- On leaving a port, the black, odd-numbered *cans* are on the port side. Think of "blackout" as a reminder.
- Mooring buoys are always white.

 ## NAVIGATIONAL CHARTS

For want of a road map, a driver may lose his way. For want of a navigational chart, a skipper may lose his boat! Far more than just showing the way, the chart is your sole guide to the depth of the water, the hazards below the surface, and the distances between ports. Always be sure you have the latest revised government chart for your area; the Coast Guard changes markers; storms and erosion may change the contours of the land; and chimneys and landmark water towers may be taken down.

Familiarize yourself with reading charts, for, although you will probably never chart a course, your aid and navigating knowledge are important when the captain's eyes and hands are busy.

 ## THE ART OF SEAMANSHIP

We strongly recommend that you study a handbook on seamanship that goes into more detail. However, seamanship encompasses far more than knowledge of the rules of the road. It also means competent boat handling and precautionary and safety habits. And that's our next chapter!

BOAT HANDLING

A first mate is second in command; as the captain's right hand she is needed everywhere at once. If you have enough helpful kids aboard, you may be able to simply pass on the orders and see that they are carried out. But in most cases, with toddlers and uncertain guests, it usually means going it alone—racing to the lines, doubling back for the fenders, and, sometimes, even fouling the halyards! To keep your captain from hysteria, learn to handle your jobs smoothly, quickly, and efficiently.

HANDLING THE LINES

Capricious winds and changing currents tense even the most experienced skipper. A smoothly thrown line, carefully gauged to be easily caught by dockside helpers, is worth an extra tot of rum. Remember, if the line misses, you may have to move off the dock and start all over again. But don't throw yourself overboard if you muff a landing—just keep practicing until you can do it smoothly.

Main Lines

These are the basic lines used by all boats. The smaller your boat, the fewer you'll need, but it's common sense and good seamanship to know all their names and uses.

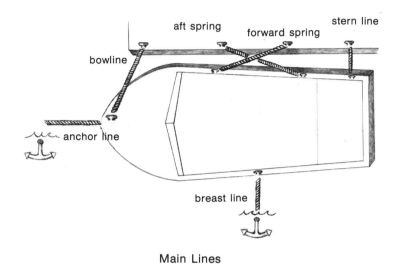

Main Lines

Pay Lines Out Smoothly

- First gather them into neat coils by passing even lengths from hand to hand.
- Take a little more than half of the coiled line (with the loop end) in your throwing hand and keep the smaller half in the other.
- Toss the larger coil to the dockside helper who will put the loop quickly on a cleat.
- Snub your end of the line to a cleat, be sure it is set into the chock, and go on to the next line to be thrown.
- Adjust the lines loosely so the boat is not tied in too closely and has length to stay clear of the dock. They can be reset more accurately later.
- For a quick guide to setting lines at your home dock, wind a strip of adhesive tape around the line at the proper length.

USEFUL KNOTS

Of course, you don't just tie a line; you make it fast. And that means using the right sailor's knot for each purpose. Below are pictured three of the most useful knots to practice until you can do them in the dark.

 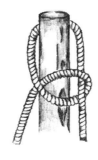 

Bowline

Clove Hitch

Cleating

FENDERS

A fender is a resilient cylinder hung from its own line to a cleat (either on the dock or deck) to protect the hull of the boat from bumping or scraping against the dock or another boat. In extremely rough weather, the captain will use a fender board, a horizontally hung length of wood that protects a larger area. The board is set in place as extra protection after the boat is securely tied up at the dock.

DEPARTING FROM THE DOCK

- Release the spring and breast lines.
- Depending on the direction of the wind and current, the captain will tell you in what order to release the other lines. Usually the stern line is first and the bow last.
- As soon as you have all the lines aboard pull up the fenders and stow them.
- Then coil the lines neatly and stow them out of the way of busy feet.

DOCKING

You will probably never dock the boat, but you should know how to do it. On a clear, calm day, practice by

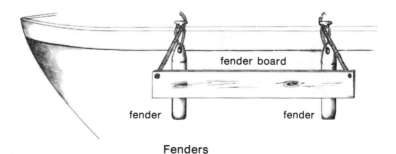

Fenders

maneuvering around a buoy. However, be well prepared to do the job you will always handle, the lines and fenders.

- Get ready beforehand by placing the fenders and coiled lines at the bow, amidships, and at the stern.
- When you are close enough to judge the length of line necessary, put out the fenders. They can be set high or low on the hull by adjusting the length of the line.
- Return to the bow and prepare to throw the line.
- When you are sure you can reach the dock, toss the line to the dockside helper.
- Make your end of the line fast to the cleat, return to the stern, and toss the second line.
- Watch the swing of the boat in the wind or current and be ready to assist in fending off a bump against the dock.
- After all lines are secure, check that each fender is properly set to keep the boat from scraping against the dock.

ANCHORING

No matter who goes forward to do the heavy anchor work, voices do not always carry over engines and wind. A set of clear, simple hand signals is important to understand and follow directions from bow to cockpit. Give signals on either side of your body, not in front where they may be hidden as you face forward. Work out motions to indicate:

move forward	turn to starboard
go faster	reverse engine
slow down	put engine into neutral gear
turn to port	cut engine

Dropping the Anchor

If you go forward to handle the anchor, use your vantage point to signal the skipper away from shallow water or rocks. Keep your eyes open while you prepare the anchor and wait for the signal to put it overboard.

- When not in use, the anchor is secured to the deck and the first step is to free it from the chocks. Check to be sure that the rode is firmly attached to the anchor ring and then fasten the loose end to a cleat.
- Upon signal from the captain, release the anchor. Never throw an anchor; you may tangle the rode or the flukes, which must always be on the underside, may not be in position to dig into the sand.
- Lower the anchor until you feel it touch bottom and then signal to reverse the engine.
- Pay out the rode as the boat falls back slowly. A small tug will set the anchor deeper. Under sail you cannot reverse the engine but, having come up against the wind or current, it will help you drift back.
- Once the anchor is firmly set and you have payed out line to about seven times the depth of the water, snub the line and signal to cut the engine.
- Take a bearing on two shore points, a tree, chimney, or house; check against them from time to time to be sure the anchor has not dragged.

Weighing Anchor

- Haul in slack line as the skipper moves the boat slowly toward the anchor.
- When slack is all taken in, tug hard to dislodge the anchor.
- If the anchor fails to come loose easily, maneuver the boat right over it, snub the line to the cleat and signal to move forward slowly until it breaks loose.
- As soon as the anchor comes free, signal for the engine to be put into neutral gear. It should remain in neutral until the anchor is on deck.

MOORING

- The skipper will head into the wind with the mooring dead ahead.
- Snare the buoy with a boathook, bring it on deck and secure the line to a cleat. If your boat has a low freeboard, you don't need the hook; simply reach down and pick up the floating buoy.

Leaving the Mooring

- Switch on the engine and keep it in neutral.
- Detach and drop the pick-up buoy.
- After the boat has drifted clear of the mooring, signal to engage the engine and move forward.

 RAFTING WITH OTHER BOATS

- With hand signals or a megaphone signal the crew on the other boat to set out their fenders and prepare to receive your lines.
- Prepare your lines and set the fenders. Because freeboards vary, tie the fender lines loosely so they will be easy to adjust later.
- Bow lines are thrown first, stern lines next.

 SMOOTH SAILING

There's a method to your skipper's madness in encouraging you to share his boating mania . . . he really needs you! That in itself should be enough incentive for you to practice, practice, practice. The reward? A great boating team.

THE SKIPPER IS BOSS

In this era of women's liberation it may be unfashionable to say it, but there is only one captain on a ship and his orders are to be obeyed. We all share the work and fun, but ultimately one person has to assume the responsibility. If you lack confidence in the skipper to the point of questioning his decisions, don't go. But if you decide to join the crew:

- Obey orders instantly.
- Never question during a maneuver. You can always ask "why" later.
- Get into the habit of repeating orders to prevent misunderstandings.
- Learn your jobs thoroughly so that you can follow commands even without thinking.

 ## SAFETY CHECKLISTS

Before You Leave the Dock

- Don't go out unless everything is in perfect working order.
- Listen to the weather report; know what's expected.
- Be sure that all the necessary charts are aboard.
- Double check that the safety equipment is in order and show your guests their location and use. Always carry: life preservers for each person aboard, fire extinguishers, a ring buoy or floating cushions in case someone goes overboard, a hand pump even on larger boats equipped with an automatic pump, and a first-aid kit and a Red Cross first-aid book.
- Leave word with someone either at home or at the dock of where you are going and when you expect to return.

SAFETY AFLOAT

Besides handling the lines, fenders, and anchor, a good first mate backstops the captain, keeping one step behind him and sometimes one ahead.

Carelessness and lack of foresight cause most accidents, and boating safety succeeds only through the cooperation and responsibility of everyone aboard. Know what to do, check as you go, and keep your eyes and ears open and your sixth sense working overtime.

⚓ BOARDING

- Don't overload your boat. Many small boats have a "capacity plate" installed by the manufacturer as a guide to the number of people and the weight that the boat can safely carry. If your boat does not carry this plate, check that the stern or bow does not ride too low in the water.
- Step, never jump, onto a boat; the motion of the water may shift the boat in the middle of your leap.

- Step into the center, not on the gunwales, of a small boat.
- Arrange your passengers so that their weight is evenly distributed.

Loading a Dinghy

- Bring the dinghy laterally alongside the bigger boat.
- Tie the bowline loosely to a cleat.
- The rower-of-the-day holds the stern line. He is the last to board and drops all lines as he does.
- Loading order; stern first, bow next, and lastly the rower onto the center seat.
- On a powered dinghy the skipper boards first and seats himself in the stern. Otherwise the loading order is the same.

Fueling

- Observe the "No Smoking" sign.
- Take portable gas tanks ashore for refueling.
- When filling tanks aboard, shut down all engines, motors, and fans.
- To avoid the accumulation of gas fumes, close all cabin hatches and portholes while refueling.
- After fueling wipe up any oil or gas spillage immediately.
- Use the bilge blower or fan to dissipate fumes that may have leaked.
- Open all cabin hatches and portholes for airing.

CRUISING

- Never allow passengers to drape themselves over the bow or gunwales while the boat is under way. Sudden veering or a strong wave might shake them overboard.

- Passengers should stay put; excessive movement can upset the boat's balance.
- Do not allow anyone to stand up in a very small boat. If one must change his position, he should crouch low and move down the center of the boat.
- Never take a wave or the wake of another boat amidships. Head into it bow on or at about a 45-degree angle.
- Never tie up to a buoy; you may obstruct it from the view of others who need it for navigation.
- Keep a sharp lookout for debris in the water. A hard knock on the rudder, props, or struts can cause severe damage and leave you out of control or adrift.
- Keep the radio tuned in and a weather eye on the barometer for changing conditions.

THE MEDICINE CHEST

One of the most important items on the boat is the American Red Cross manual of first-aid remedies. Keep it handy, learn the methods of resuscitation, and make sure all the crew can practice lifesaving methods.

The medical supplies on a boat are generally the same necessities you keep at home—sterile pads, adhesives, and antiseptics. The only extras suggested are needles and tweezers for deck and dock splinters and seasick pills for queasy stomachs. Always carry a good supply of suntan lotion and a preparation to relieve the discomfort of a burn.

Ask your family physician for suggestions on emergency supplies for burns and severe cuts and for pain killers to use until you can get to a doctor.

- Buy your medicines and toiletries in plastic bottles and jars when possible.
- Keep duplicate bottles aboard of any special medicines. You may forget to bring the prescription when you pack.

- If you have difficulty spotting a splinter, a drop of iodine will outline it clearly.
- For painless splinter surgery, press an ice cube to the spot.
- Fresh air is the best medicine for a queasy stomach at sea. The rolling motion is exaggerated below deck, so keep the sufferer topside. Tell him to breathe deeply and to keep his eyes on a fixed point. A dry cracker or a piece of bread also helps to settle a nervous stomach. If possible, let the victim take a turn at the wheel. It has a stabilizing effect.

 ## EMERGENCY PROCEDURES

Even with the best equipment and a clear knowledge of proper procedures, a panicky crew racing about in an emergency causes havoc. The missing ingredient is discipline. Only training will control a potential tragedy.

Basic Emergency Rules

- Everyone on board must keep calm.
- Everyone goes to his assigned task.
- Radio or signaling devices are activated.
- Emergency equipment, fire extinguishers, pails, and life rings are made ready.
- One person passes out life preservers.
- The crew proceeds to an assembly station and stays out of the way.

Man Overboard Drill

- Throw the engine into neutral until the swimmer is clear of the boat. More people have been injured by propellers than have drowned by falling overboard.
- One person, previously designated, tosses the *unattached* ring buoy (or cushion) near, *not at,* the swimmer.

- The stern of the boat is swung away from the swimmer as it circles to return.
- As soon as the approach has been made and the boat is close to the swimmer—allowing for drift in wind and current—put the engine in neutral.
- If the freeboard of the boat is low, there is danger of capsizing while assisting the swimmer aboard. To balance the pull, move the other passengers to the opposite side of the cockpit.
- Tow the swimmer to shore if it is too difficult or dangerous to bring him aboard.

Fire Drill

- In the event of fire the skipper will shut off all engines and fuel lines and try to steer the boat into the wind so it does not fan the flames.
- The rest of the crew goes to preassigned tasks.
- Hatches and portholes are closed to cut off the wind.
- Fire extinguishers are manned.
- Pails are filled with water from over the side.
- Life preservers are passed out.
- If the fire is in the stern or amidships, everyone not assigned to firefighting goes to the bow. If the fire is in the bow section, they assemble in the stern.
- Everyone remains at the assembly point until the fire is under control or the order to abandon ship is given.

Abandon Ship Drill

- At the emergency signal, everyone checks his life preserver and goes to a preassigned station.
- No one leaves the boat until the captain gives the order.
- At the command, everyone pairs off with a preassigned buddy; a strong swimmer with a weaker one, a young child

with a parent. In pairs, everyone goes overboard.
- Once in the water, all assemble near the bow.
- Help rescuers find you by staying together and near the boat. However, if the ship is on fire, move at least 30 yards off because of the danger of explosion.
- Do not attempt to swim to shore; you may misjudge the distance or your stamina.

How to Call for Help

The Coast Guard is constantly alert for distress signals, and operators of pleasure boats are required to offer aid to any vessel in distress. Here's how to attract attention:

- Shoot signal flares.
- Fly flags at half mast or upside down, the recognized distress signal.
- Stand on the highest point of the boat and repeatedly raise and lower your outstretched arms.
- Wrap aluminum foil around the mast or on a pole to aid radar-equipped boats in their search.
- Follow ship-to-shore radio procedures: Turn to the Coast Guard channel 2182. Break in on any conversation by using the words "May Day." Give your name, call letters, position, and nature of the problem. Switch back for reply. If there is no answer, continue to call, repeating the information. Check back for a reply each time the message is completed.

These rules and drills will soon become second nature. And everyone has a few of his own. That's what seamanship is all about; the ability to think clearly, to adapt quickly, and to handle situations competently.

WEATHER WATCHING

No outdoor activity depends on the weather so completely as boating. Threatening weather rarely cancels a game of golf or tennis, but no sensible boating family puts out to sea or stays out if there is a chance of heavy rain or high winds. Getting back to shore in foul weather can be a dusty trip.

STAY AHEAD OF WEATHER CHANGES

The one constant fact about weather is that it changes—and often. Here's how to keep up:

- Obtain the weather forecast before you set out.
- Know where storm-warning flags are flown in your area and watch for changes.
- Learn the weather clues in the sky, in clouds, and on shore.

- Carry a portable or marine radio and tune in for weather reports as you cruise.
- Check your own weather instruments for weather shifts.

✸ FORECASTS

With line squalls whipping out of nowhere and fig swirling in without warning, seafarers of old had a rough time with weather changes. We have access to detailed weather information from TV, newspapers, and Coast Guard and National Weather Service broadcasts. To find the station settings and hours of the broadcasts, write to the Coast Guard station in your area for their pamphlet, "Marine Communication for the Boating Public" and to the National Weather Service (either in Washington, D.C., or in your area) for their "Coastal Warnings Facilities Chart."

✸ WEATHER LANGUAGE

Weather forecasts won't help much unless you understand the weatherman's language and why each observation is important.

- Wind direction refers to the point *from* which the wind moves; an easterly wind comes from the east and a westerly wind from the west.
- An offshore breeze blows out to sea; an onshore wind moves in from the water.
- Wind shifts move in a clockwise direction; if the wind is from the north, it will next shift to the east.
- The prevailing winds in the United States are westerly. So weather conditions move with the wind from the Pacific coast to the Atlantic. However, winds vary in each locale; West Coast local winds coming off the Pacific usually bring rain, the opposing easterlies off the coastal mountains bring

clearing skies. On the East Coast, the effect of the wind direction is reversed; east winds from the Atlantic bring foul weather, and the westerlies from shore mean fair weather in store.

- Wind velocity describes the miles or knots per hour at which the wind moves and the speed of the weather changes it is bringing.
- Weather bureaus measure wind velocity in knots; 1 knot or nautical mile equals 1.13 miles. A 10-knot breeze is travelling at 11.3 mph.
- The National Weather Service has classified wind velocity: 1–7 knots, light winds; 8–12 knots, gentle winds; 12–18 knots, moderate winds; 19–24 knots, fresh winds; 25–40 knots, strong or gale winds.
- Wind velocity also affects the surface of the water. A strong wind some distance away creates long, high swells that signal the approach of a storm even before the sky or barometer shows any warning. Winds of 22 knots or more may whip up rough seas that are hazardous for small boats.
- The Beaufort Scale, a scale of wind velocity described in "forces," was established in 1805 by Sir Francis Beaufort. This first scale of wind velocity is still used by large vessels at sea.
- Air pressure indicates the density of the atmosphere. Changes signal weather shifts. In general, a falling barometer means foul weather; a rising barometer brings clear blue skies. If the rise is slow and steady, good weather will settle in for a while.
- Fog, the boatsman's scourge, forms when warm air moves over a colder surface. It is borne by the wind from one area to another. It remains until the sun warms the fog bank and evaporates the moisture.

YOUR WEATHER INSTRUMENTS

Rely on your own instrument readings even if they do not agree with the official forecast. Remember that the latter is

Wind Velocity and Sea Condition

Terms used by U.S. Weather Bureau	Velocity m.p.h.	Velocity knots	Estimating velocities on sea	Probable mean height of waves in feet*	Description of sea
Calm	Less than 1	Less than 1	Sea like a mirror.		Calm (glassy)
Light	1–3	1–3	Ripples with the appearance of scales are formed but without foam crests.	½	Rippled
	4–7	4–6	Small wavelets, still short but more pronounced, crests have a glassy appearance and do not break	1	Smooth
Gentle	8–12	7–10	Large wavelets. Crests begin to break. Foam of glassy appearance. Perhaps scattered white caps.	2½	
Moderate	13–18	11–16	Small waves, becoming longer; fairly frequent white caps.	5	Slight
Fresh	19–24	17–21	Moderate waves, taking a more pronounced long form; many white caps are formed. (Chance of some spray.)	10	Moderate
Strong	25–31	22–27	Large waves begin to form; the white foam crests are more extensive everywhere. (Probably some spray.)	15	Rough
	32–38	28–33	Sea heaps up and white foam from breaking waves begins to be blown in streaks along the direction of the wind.	20	Very rough
	39–46	34–40	Moderately high waves of greater length; edges of crests break into spindrift. The foam is blown in well-marked streaks along the direction of the wind.	25	High

Wind Velocity and Sea Condition (Continued)

Terms used by U.S. Weather Bureau	Velocity m.p.h.	Velocity knots	Estimating velocities on sea	Probable mean height of waves in feet*	Description of sea
Gale	47–54	41–47	High waves. Dense streaks of foam along the direction of the wind. Sea begins to roll. Spray may affect visibility.	30	
	55–63	48–55	Very high waves with long, overhanging crests. The resulting foam, in great patches, is blown in dense white streaks along the direction of the wind. On the whole, the surface of the sea takes on a white appearance. The rolling of the sea becomes heavy and shocklike. Visibility is affected.	35	Very high
Whole Gale	64–73	56–63	Exceptionally high waves. (Small and medium-sized ships might for a long time be lost to view behind the waves.) The sea is completely covered with long white patches of foam lying along the direction of the wind. Everywhere edges of the wave crests are blown into froth. Visibility affected.	40	
Hurricane	74–82	64–71	The air is filled with foam and spray. Sea completely white with driving spray; visibility very seriously affected.	45 or more.	Phenomenal

*Height in open seas with time for wind to build waves.

a *general* survey of the weather but cannot be specific enough to warn of local squalls that surprise the unwary sailor. To be on the safe side, get into the habit of checking your own weather instruments.

- If the forecast is clear but your barometer takes a dip, a local storm is brewing.
- Some larger boats carry an anemometer to measure local wind velocity and keep tabs on changing weather patterns.
- The wind sock on a sailboat mast and the flags and pennants on a power boat show wind direction at a glance. Roosting seagulls and anchored boats always face into the wind and also show wind direction. To identify the direction, check the compass.

STORM WARNING FLAGS

The National Weather Service uses the visual storm-warning system of red and black flags by day and red and white lights at night to warn of present or predicted weather hazards. These storm warnings are posted in marinas, yacht clubs, and Coast Guard installations. Even on a clear day keep a watch on the flags—weather changes rapidly.

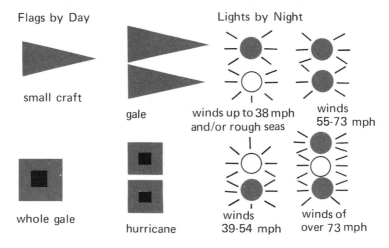

Flags by Day
Lights by Night

small craft

gale

winds up to 38 mph and/or rough seas

winds 55-73 mph

whole gale

hurricane

winds 39-54 mph

winds of over 73 mph

⚓ READING THE SKY

A mackerel sky with mare's tails
Makes tall ships carry low sails.
Red sky at morning, sailor take warning.
Red sky at night, sailor's delight.

Ancient mariners looked to the sky to interpret changing weather patterns and really saw the mackerel scales and mare's tails in the rhymes. The mare's tails are long plumes of very white clouds; the mackerel scales look just like fish scales.

They knew, too, that a rainbow signals one of two very different weather patterns. Seen in the morning, it brings rain later in the day, but, if it appears in the afternoon, fair weather will continue.

The Color of the Sky

- bright blue—fair weather
- vivid red at sunset—fair tomorrow
- vivid red at sunrise—foul weather
- grey and dull at sunset—foul tomorrow

Cloud Formations

- fleecy light clouds—fair
- small dark clouds—rain
- streaks and patches of white clouds after fair weather—bad weather ahead, wind or rain
- heavy clouds moving toward you—storm near
- squall lines move at about 20 to 30 knots per hour—a storm on the horizon will reach your position in about an hour

Appearance of the Sun and Moon

- ring around the moon—stormy tomorrow
- weak, washed-out sun—rain probable
- glaring white at sunset—storm coming
- red ball at sunset—fair tomorrow

Fog and Haze

- continuing haze, no clouds, little wind—probable fog
- fog lifting slowly in the morning—fog and rain will return
- fog clearing early in the morning—weather fair

Changes on Shore

- leaves blowing with the undersides out—wind bringing rain
- birds flying low or perched on wires—low pressure, weather changing
- insects flying low, hitting the car windshield as you drive to the dock—low pressure, weather changing
- chimney smoke rising straight into the air—fair weather
- chimney smoke flat or streaming off to the side—low pressure, storm coming

WEATHER FORECASTING

Forecasting is one of the skills a boating family develops. It works anywhere and anytime and soon becomes intuitive. No one has come up with a way of conquering the elements, but it's good to know you can keep ahead of a brewing storm.

IN THE WAKE

SECTION VI

DO-IT-YOURSELF: SANDING, PAINTING, AND VARNISHING

CHAPTER 19

Painting is one of the most important steps in maintenance. Even ashore, wood must be protected from the elements and, at sea, it is much more important. Exterior painting is usually left to the man on board, but there will be interior paint jobs for you.

All paint stores are ready with advice, so pick your dealer's brains on what to use and how to use it to be sure your boat is always "fresh as paint."

SANDING COMES FIRST

A new coat of paint or varnish won't adhere smoothly unless the surface has been sanded. Light sanding may be all that is needed if the surface requires only one coat of paint, but check for nicks and gouges to smooth or for a heavy buildup of paint. Paint and varnish will flake, bubble, or check after too many coats have been applied. If any of these conditions are present, the surface must be sanded down to bare wood before repainting.

Equipment for Sanding

- Rent a sanding machine for the big jobs where there is a heavy buildup or a large area to be prepared. The time and work you save is easily worth the rental fee.
- For smaller areas, use a hand sanding block, an oblong piece of wood with slots in the sides to hold the paper in place.
- Use coarse sandpaper for the tough job of removing old paint and getting down to bare wood, medium paper to take off a coat of paint or two and smooth rough spots. Fine sandpaper is always used after heavy and medium paper to give the final, smooth surface.

How to Work

- It is not necessary to press hard.
- Use firm, even strokes.
- Sand in one direction for a smoother job.
- When running a sanding machine, cover your mouth and nose with a mask. The machine kicks up a mountain of dust.
- Fine grains of paint and wood dust make a mess of new paint so, after sanding, clean the surface thoroughly. Use a vacuum cleaner and follow up with a cloth dampened with turpentine.

WHEN TO USE PAINT REMOVER

A thick paint base must eventually be taken down to bare wood. It is a long, tedious job even with a machine; it is easier with a chemical paint remover. In addition to the remover you will need a paint brush, scraper, rubber gloves, and neutralizer.

- Always wear rubber gloves—the remover is very caustic.
- Lavishly brush on the remover, one area (about three feet by three feet) at a time.

- Wait at least 15 to 20 minutes for the surface to begin to bubble and blister before scraping.
- Scrape off the loosened paint with firm, even strokes of the scraper. Don't press too hard or you may gouge the wood.
- Apply a second coat if the surface is heavily builtup.
- When you are halfway through one section, take time out to prepare the next so that it will be blistered and ready when you get to it.
- When you have finished the entire area, use the neutralizer according to directions.
- Sand out the nicks with coarse or medium sandpaper and finish off with a fine grade of paper to prepare for painting.

 PAINTING

It is false economy to skimp on paint; always use the best quality available. Try the water-soluble paints for interior jobs. They are fast drying, are easy to apply, and have little odor. Best of all, a quick water rinse cleans the brush in a jiffy.

Even on the most perfectly maintained boat, covering up interior leaks usually leaves tell tale spots that *look* touched up. To avoid patches;

- Buy premixed colors of popular brands of paint and keep a record of the color *and* number so you can get the exact mixture again.
- If you prefer mixing your own colors, measure carefully and keep a record of the exact proportions.

At last you're ready for painting. Well, almost. First:

- Clean up the entire area.
- Be sure the surface to be painted is dry and free of dust or grease.
- Take a weather and time check before you start. Moisture in the air will *pit* the new coat; both dampness and night air will delay drying.

- Set your paint can on a paper plate to catch the drippings.
- Stir the paint well to be sure that there are no lumps and that the color is uniform.

Painting Procedures

- Paint in sections, using even strokes.
- Paint from the top of the bulkhead to the bottom so you won't drip or brush against a newly finished section.
- Go easy on dipping into the paint bucket. Thickly applied paint leaves telltale brush strokes.
- Apply the paint against the grain of the wood and then go back and brush lightly with the grain to smooth it out.
- When starting an adjacent area, don't be afraid to overlap the edge of the finished section. Featherlight strokes in the same direction will smooth and blend the edges.

 VARNISHING

Varnish is a resinous substance painted over bare or stained wood to produce a clear, hard finish aptly known as brightwork. Nothing gives a boat that touch of luxury, that "yachty" look, so much as gleaming brightwork built up to a high gloss. There is less and less varnish on newer boats but if you are lucky enough to have some, give it tender loving care.

- For brightwork in good condition, a light sanding with fine paper and one coat of varnish will usually bring the wood back to a beautiful glow. However, if you must begin with bare wood three or four coats are necessary to start. Then over the months build up to five or six coats.
- If the varnished area is stained or blistered, sand it down to bare wood, just as if you were going to paint.
- Bleach out stains and black spots with oxalic acid or hydrogen peroxide, both available in drugstores. Rinse off the solution with water.

- Clean the prepared surface thoroughly with a cloth dampened with turpentine.
- Never stir varnish in the can. It produces bubbles that often cannot be brushed out.
- Dip the brush carefully into the can, again, to prevent bubbles.
- Use long, flowing evenly applied, strokes.
- Brush strokes show very clearly in varnish, so don't use too much on the brush.
- If any bubbles do appear, brush them quickly and gently away. Brush them toward the undone section so they can escape.
- Watch for *holidays* (missed spots) and go over them promptly. Varnish becomes sticky and tacky very fast, and it is difficult to go over mistakes if they are left to dry.
- If more than one coat is necessary, the first coat must be completely dry before starting the next.
- Sand lightly and dust well before applying the next coat. The sanded area will look whitish and terrible but only until you apply your brush.

If it all sounds like a lot of work, you're right! But it's worth every bit of effort when you hear someone say, "Now *that's* a beautiful boat!"

DAY BOATS

Many of the craft that swell boating statistics are small sail or power day boats. More and more of a new breed of rugged yachtsmen, the campers, are finding ways to use their small day boats for more than the picnicking, skiiing, or fishing for which they were designed. With the additions of camping equipment and portable galley gear, they trailer their boats to the many protected rivers and lakes that are too shallow for larger boats.

The official maritime definition of a yacht is a pleasure boat over 16 feet, and that certainly includes day boats that run up to 22 feet in length. Despite the official designation there is precious little room for cruising accommodations. Both power and sailing day boats may have tiny V berths forward, a hideaway head, and that's about all. Many don't even have that.

The power boats, generally known as runabouts, are usually fitted with a folding canvas top to provide shade.

Throughout this book, one theme has been finding space. But because of the acute space problems on day boats they deserve this special chapter.

⚙ MAKING ROOM

You really don't need a ton of equipment to prepare for your camping expedition, but you must stow far more gear than your boat was designed to carry. You must find room for cruising supplies, sleeping gear, galleyware, and clothing and linens. Make the best use of the space you have and improvise to create storage areas where none existed.

- The forward forepeak, or cuddy, is the one enclosed area built into the boat. You can't afford to let the crew toss in gear at will. Fit the sides with hooks and shelves to hang ditty bags and supplies neatly out of the way. Be firm about everyone returning his gear to a specific hook.
- Enclose the open space beneath built-in benches with sliding plywood doors to make an extra storage bin. If you

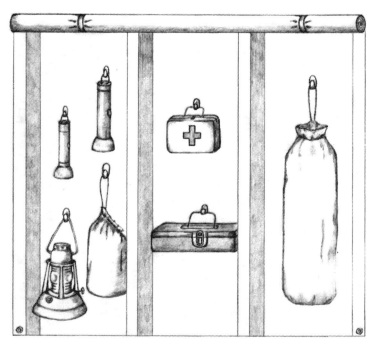

Extra Storage in Cockpit

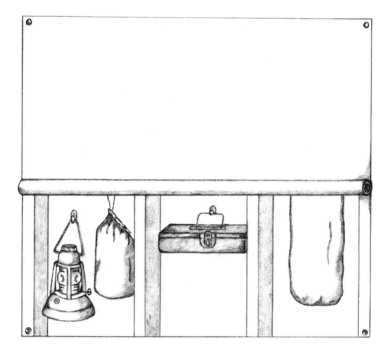

plan an active camping season, it may be worth the investment of rearranging and adding benches so as to create as much storage and seating space as possible.

• When the ribs on the sides of the boat are exposed, the open spaces can be fitted with hooks and narrow shelves. Everything can be stowed neatly out of the way without even being seen by attaching a protective piece of canvas or sailcloth secured with snaps or ties to keep gear dry from rain or spray.

SAFETY AND CRUISING SUPPLIES

The checklists of safety and cruising supplies in other chapters hold true for a small boat, too. Of course, you will cut down to basics. The only extra equipment needed is an oar or paddle to be used in the event the engine quits and extra heavy-duty flashlights.

 OVERNIGHT TRIPS

There are established campsites with extensive facilities in most national and state parks. A phone call to local recreational authorities or a park ranger will answer your questions. Each site has its own regulations, but these are universal:

- Don't camp outside designated areas unless you have permission.
- Leave plenty of room between your campsite and the next.
- Don't be a nuisance by borrowing equipment or making noise.
- Be sure to clean up your area when you leave.

As in a marina, boating campers must follow the rules. Courtesy and good sportsmanship will always make you welcome.

IMPROVISE A PORTABLE GALLEY

An ice chest, a portable stove, and a large cutting board —plus a little ingenuity—can create an efficient galley on the boat or at a campsite ashore.

- When in use aboard, hook the stove onto gimbals on the outside of the boat, out of the way of the engine. Any accident with the flames will go into the water, not on the deck.
- The cutting board serves as counter space during preparations.
- Adapt the customized picnic basket (p.73) to hold all the cooking and table utensils.
- Organize two sturdy wooden boxes (that double for seating) to compactly stow galleyware; one box to hold cooking

utensils and the other to store unrefrigerated foods and galley essentials.

- Refer to the galley chapters for guidelines on equipping and stocking your portable galley, cutting the lists to basics.
- Buy stainless steel or camping equipment for greater durability.
- The only extras you will need are a dishpan and plastic bottles or jerry cans for water.
- An easy way to carry all your herbs and spices is to transfer small amounts from your stores at home to plastic pill vials. Put the labels on the inside of the vial so they won't peel off in damp air.
- Plan on simple, hearty meals, using packaged and dehydrated foods. A good bedtime snack is hot bouillon (from cubes) and crackers.
- Double wrap dry goods in aluminum foil to protect them from damp air.

SLEEPING OUTDOORS

Your day boat becomes a sleeper just by using sleeping bags. If your city bones can't take the hard life, bring along air mattresses. Pretest the mattresses before you settle down for the night; if they are too soft you'll feel the deck or ground beneath you; if too full, you'll bounce uncomfortably.

It's great to sleep under the stars, but what happens on a rainy night? A tent, bought or rented, is one answer. A less expensive solution is to insert poles into holders screwed to the hull of the boat and to spread a canvas shelter over them. Both coverings are quickly rigged and compactly stored.

CLOTHING AND LINENS

When you use sleeping bags, face and swimming towels are the only extra linens you'll need. Take along enough

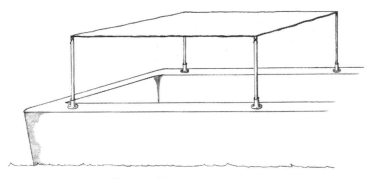

Canvas Shelter for Deck

but dole them out like pearls. The ready bags (detailed on p. 75) are perfect organizers for cruising on a small boat. Make them in any size you need for clothing and linens and hang them in the forepeak. Each crew member may have his own ready bag for his personal gear, toilet kit, and books. Be sure to label each bag conspicuously to avoid confusion. Check the clothing list on p. 83 and, again, cut it down.

DITTY BAG

A ditty bag is a sailor's knapsack, chock full of the odds and ends needed on long trips to sea. And that's what is packed into this ditty bag—all the bits of boating lore and information that often crop up.

⚓ BOAT NOTES

- Remember the adage, "one hand for the boat and one for yourself." Always find a handrail or handhold.
- Keep your valuables in a watertight metal box in a "secret" place on board. Wrap the box in a watertight plastic covering and use it to store your money or traveler's checks, ship's papers, and credit cards.
- "May Day," the universal call for help, is the americanization of the French words, *"m'aidez,"* help me.
- The Power Squadron is a nonprofit organization devoted to boating safety, education, navigation, and co-operation with the government in formulating boating

laws and regulations. Apply to your local squadron for public courses given by volunteer instructors.

• The United States Coast Guard Auxiliary was established by Congress in 1939, and it holds similar aims and purposes with the Power Squadron. Its membership is composed of civilians under the direction and supervision of the Coast Guard. Membership is not restricted to yachtsmen but also includes airplane pilots and radio "hams," all of whom can aid the Coast Guard in emergency operations. Among other services, the Auxiliary offers courtesy examinations to volunteering skippers to check that their boats carry all equipment required for each class boat and to ensure that all safety precautions are followed. The Auxiliary also gives boating courses; you can consult your local headquarters for information.

CLASS BOATS

Boats are classified and grouped by length: Class A includes boats up to 16 feet; Class 1 boats are 16 feet to 26 feet; Class 2 goes to 40 feet; and Class 3 includes those up to 60 feet. These classifications are important, because they determine the kinds of equipment and lights required by maritime law that each must carry.

DESIGNS OF SAILBOATS AND POWER BOATS

Even if you are a "stinkpot" enthusiast, a sailboat under full canvas is a lovely sight. And an ardent sailor can appreciate a sleek power boat moving gracefully through the water. Part of everyone's boating education includes knowing the difference between the rigs on sailboats and power boat designs.

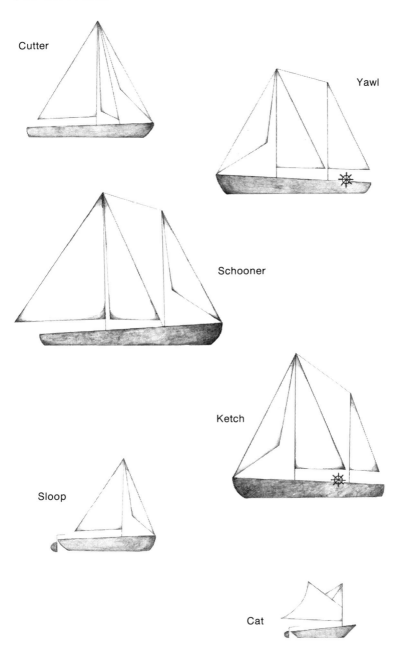

Cutter

Yawl

Schooner

Ketch

Sloop

Cat

Sailboats

Catboat. one mast with one sail

Sloop. one mast with two sails, mainsail and jib

Cutter. one mast, mainsail, and at least two headsails

Yawl. two masts, the larger one forward and the smaller one aft of the wheel

Ketch. two masts, a smaller mainsail, and a larger mizzen than a yawl. The mizzen on a ketch is forward of the wheel.

Schooner. two masts, the shorter one forward and the mainsail aft

Power Boats

Day cruiser. an expanded version of a runabout with a bare minimum of accommodations. They usually provide V berths forward and a small head.

Sportfisherman. specially designed for fishing with a large aft cockpit for fishing chairs and gear. The cabins are small with just basic comforts.

Sedan. a cruising boat with the cabins on the same level as the cockpit. The cockpit space is smaller than a sportfisherman to allow for larger cabins.

Double Cabin Flying Bridge (DCFB). a boating version of the split-level house. It is a more luxurious boat with two or more staterooms and a main salon. The fly bridge is the deck, on top of the aft cabin, from which the boat is piloted.

Houseboat. a flat hull, low on the water, on which the housing is built, usually powered by outboard engines. Because of the room and comforts they provide, houseboats have been booming in popularity.

Other Designs

Motorsailor. a combination of power and sail, has the more comfortable living features of power boats with the sailing features of a sailboat. The sails are used at sea when the wind is up, but in calm weather and in maneuvering in harbors, power is used.

Catamaran. a double-hulled craft joined by a strong, flat center piece. They come in many models and sizes and may be fitted with either sails or power. They are unusually stable and fast.

Trimaran. similar to a catamaran but with three hulls for greater stability.

READING THE WATER

A close study of the water's appearance can give you important clues about depth, hidden obstacles, and even good fishing ground.

- Deep water is usually a darker color. Shallow water is light green or blue and ripples more readily when the wind comes up.
- Eddies, ripples, and other breaks and swirls in the current of a river or running tide at sea may indicate hidden obstacles below the water. Stay clear.
- Feeding pelicans, hovering gulls, and jumping fish are clues that you've found a good fishing ground.

SHIP'S TIME

Ship's time is measured in the four-hour "watch" periods when crew members change shifts. Watches are observed when a boat makes a long voyage with no overnight stops. All nautical clocks strike the hours in ship's time. Two bells signal the start of each watch so the sequence is repeated every four hours around the clock.

2 bells — 1:00	2 bells — 5:00	2 bells — 9:00
4 bells — 2:00	4 bells — 6:00	4 bells — 10:00
6 bells — 3:00	6 bells — 7:00	6 bells — 11:00
8 bells — 4:00	8 bells — 8:00	8 bells — 12:00

⚓ FLAGS

Flag etiquette is an integral part of boating courtesy with its own protocol for when and where the flags should be displayed.

- To "dress ship" means to put out flags from stem to stern for racing, yachting events, and special holidays.
- The hours of display for all flags are from 8:00 A.M. to sundown.
- The American flag (ensign) is always flown from the stern of power boats and from the after peak (the top of the aft-mast) on sailing vessels.
- Display your burgee (triangular yacht club flag) on the bow or foremast.
- Fly the owner's flag (designed by and for the boat owner) from the mast only when he is aboard.
- If you are lucky enough to visit a foreign land, it is a courteous gesture to fly the ensign of your host country from the masthead.

⚓ RACING

If you travel with racing enthusiasts, you already know the big races, but, even if you don't follow the circuit, you may want to follow the conversation!

- The America's Cup, the most famous international racing event, was begun by England in 1851. The annual competition is between the United States and challenging foreign 12-meter sailing yachts. If there is more than one challenger, elimination races are run to narrow the final race to two boats. The trophy is a silver cup, originally called the Hundred Guinea cup, donated by the Royal Yacht Squadron of England. After the United States won the trophy in the original race, it became known as the America's Cup, and competition to take it has attracted worldwide interest.

There were no races during the war years. In recent years the competition has been held off Newport, Rhode Island.

- The Gold Cup, sponsored by the American Power Boat Association for boats 40 feet, and under, is the most important power-boat racing event in the country. In existence since 1904, the sites of the races have been changed from the East Coast to the West Coast. The winner is determined not only by speed but by endurance; the course can run to 32 nautical miles. Today speeds of up to 160 mph are reached. The boats, owned by large companies or by teams with sponsors, are manned by professional drivers. Many technical advances for power boats have been developed by the builders of these competition boats.
- Predicted log racing—after a course is given, the skipper estimates the time it will take his boat to cover the course. Then, without clock of distance measuring devices, he tries to match his estimate. The one who comes closest wins.

GLOSSARY

Aft toward the rear of the boat

Aground touching bottom

All hands everyone in the crew

Amidships center (lengthwise) of a boat

Anchor any heavy implement that holds the boat in one place

Anchor flukes pointed extensions of the anchor which dig into the sand

Anchor rode line connecting the anchor to the boat

Anchorage sheltered spot to anchor a boat

Anemometer instrument for measuring wind velocity

Automatic pilot automatic steering system to keep a boat on course without the need of a helmsman

Bail to dip water out of a boat

Barnacle marine crustacean that fixes itself to the hull of a boat or dock piling

Barometer instrument to measure air pressure

Battens thin, flexible strips of wood used to stiffen the edges of a sail

Beach (a boat) to run or haul a boat onto shore

Beam width of the boat amidships

Belay to make turns with the line around a cleat

Below below the deck or inside the boat

Berth docking place, or a bunk or bed

Bilge inside of a hull below the waterline

Bilge pump pump (automatic or hand) used to remove water from the inside of the boat

Binnacle casing or covering for the compass

Bitt fixed post on the deck to secure lines

Boarding ladder lightweight ladder hung over the side of a boat for boarding

Boarding platform shelf attached to the transom of a boat, a few inches above the water line, used in boarding from the water or a dinghy

Boathook pole with a hook at the end used to fend off or to retrieve objects from the water or to pick up a mooring line

Bollard fixed post attached to the dock to secure lines.

Boom on a sailboat, a pole that extends the foot of a sail; moves from side to side with the sail

Boom crutch support for the boom to keep it in place when not in use

Boot top painted strip around the boat just above the water line

Borer sea organism that bores into and eats wood on the hull

Bottom exterior hull of the boat that is under water

Bow forward part of the boat

Bow line line used to tie up the forward part of the boat to the dock

Bow rail safety railing around the bow of the boat

Bowsprit extension over and forward of the bow. Used when handling sails or fishing

Breach the boat's rolling over by the wind or waves

Break out prepare for use

Bridge the area from which a power boat is piloted

Brightwork varnished woodwork

Bulkhead dividing partition (wall) below decks

Bumper fender

Buoy numbered, floating aid to navigation, installed and maintained by the Coast Guard

Burgee triangular or swallow-tailed flag of a yacht club

Calk or caulk to force material into the seams of a hull or deck to make it watertight

Canvas sails; also, a protective covering

Carry to have on board

Cast off to let go, to set sail

Chafing gear   cloth, canvas, or rubber buffers to lessen or prevent rubbing and wearing of lines

Channel   deepest part of a body of water, marked by buoys, which boats use as a "road"

Chock   fitting with a slot, through which to run a line

Cleat   fitting with a stem and two horns to which to secure lines

Close-hauled   with sails as flat as possible

Close to the wind   sailing with the bow close to the direction from which the wind is coming

Cockpit   area from which to pilot a sailboat

Come about   change the course of the boat

Commission   prepare for launching

Companionway   steps leading from the dock to the cabin

Davits   cranes used to raise or lower a dinghy or other heavy object

Deck   interior or exterior floors

Depth finder   instrument to measure the depth of the water

Dinghy   small open boat carried or stowed by a larger boat

Dink   slang for dinghy

Dock   platform to which to secure a boat

Draft   depth of a boat below the water line

Ensign   flag carried by a boat to show the country of registry

Fend off   to hold off, to push off

Fender   device used to protect the side of the boat from contact with a dock or another boat

Fittings   hardware secured to the boat

Fore   toward the bow of the boat

Forward   bow section

Foul   to entangle

Freeboard   distance from gunwale to water line

Gear   term for all items used in operating a boat or needed by those aboard

Generator   auxiliary engine that produces electricity to start the engine, supply lights, and charge the batteries

Gimbal   device to keep things level on a boat—compass, stove, rings to hold glasses, and tables

Grab rail   railing placed at various points about the boat to be grasped to steady a person

Gunwhale   (pronounced gunnal)—the upper edge of the side of the boat where the topside meets the deck

Hailer   powered megaphone to amplify the voice

Halyard   rope to hoist and lower a sail or a flag

Hatch   opening (a door or a porthole) to give access to the interior of a boat

Head   boat's toilet or bathroom

Headway   forward movement

Heel   tilt of a boat pushed by the wind, waves, or a heavy weight on one side

Helm   steering apparatus

Home port   port in which the boat is kept or from which it sails

Housing   superstructure on the boat; cabin or deckhouse

Hull   body of the boat

Keel   backbone of the boat's hull, running from stem to stern

Knot   unit of speed

Lee   sheltered side off the shore; sheltered from the wind

Line   ropes

Make fast   tie up

Marina   boat basin equipped with docks (slips) and facilities for fuel, water, and supplies

Mast   long upright poles on which sails are mounted

Mooring   area where a boat is kept, whether at a dock or anchorage; *a* mooring is a heavy anchor permanently set. It has a floating marker that is taken on board to secure the boat.

Off   away from

Pay out   to let out, as line

Port   left side of a boat when facing forward; also a harbor

Porthole   round opening (with a hinged cover) on the side of a boat to let in light and air

Pulpit   platform that extends over and forward of the bow on a power boat; used on fishing boats to facilitate bringing in large game fish

Put in   to enter a harbor

Radio Direction Finder (RDF)   electronic device to aid in determining the boat's position through the use of radio signals transmitted from points ashore

Raft up   two or more boats tying up together

Rendezvous   group of boats meeting at a specified place

Ribs   frames of the boat hull

Rode   line connecting the anchor to the boat

Rudder   flat plate mounted under the stern; steers the boat when turned with the action of the pilot wheel or helm

Salon, Saloon   main cabin of a boat

Screw   slang for propeller

Secure   tie up

Slack   loose line

Snub   to halt a line that is running out by turning it around a bitt or a cleat

Stand off   steer away from

Starboard   right side of the boat when facing forward

Stem to stern   entire length of the boat from bow to transom

Stern   rear part of the boat

Stow   to store away

Telltale   bit of string or ribbon tied to a sailboat shroud to show the direction of the wind

Topside   sides of the hull between the waterline and the deck railings; also, out on deck

Trailer   metal frame on wheels with which to transport a small boat behind an automobile

Transom   flat planking of the stern hull

Trim   set of the sails; also balance of the boat. When floating in the water the boat should float evenly on the waterline. If it does not, it is off trim.

Under way   not tied up or at anchor

Wake   path of water left astern by the forward motion of the boat

Weigh anchor   to lift the anchor; to set out

Winch   mechanism designed to aid in the hauling and winding of ropes and lines

Wind sock   open-ended conical tube of light material attached to the top of a mast to show wind direction

INDEX